NOBODY WANTS TO LISTEN - AND YET!

by
Sir Oliver Lodge

Spiritually Transcribed
by
Raymond Smith

Illustrations by Richard E. Baddeley

CON-PSY PUBLICATIONS MIDDLESEX

First Edition

© Raymond Smith
1995

ISBN 1 898680 04 3

Published by

CON-PSY PUBLICATIONS

**22 KINGSLEY AVENUE
SOUTHALL
MIDDLESEX UB1 2NA**

CONTENTS

TESTIMONIALS

ROY AND ANNETTE BUTTON

We have been fortunate to witness the culmination of this most inspiring and enlightening book and have an exciting feeling about the impact it will have on its readers.

Having lived in close proximity to the co-author for many years and enjoyed many, many hours of stimulating communication from Sir Oliver Lodge and the other members of the group who have now become almost like family, we feel privileged to be asked to contribute to the foreword of this genuine and remarkable book which, in essence, leaves no stone unturned where knowledge and wisdom prevail. Many of the teachings have been expressed to give simplistic understanding and yet are profoundly impressive. Truly inspiring. An ascension in wisdom.

ALBERT AND GWEN TISCH

Early in the 1980's, my wife and I sat with Ray and June Smith, along with their daughter and a friend in his home in Sussex. After a short period of time, it gradually became apparent that the object of this circle was to develop Ray's gifts. After a few weeks he was not entranced, but had instant recall of the words that had been passing through his mind. The recall was amazing in as much as the lectures were of a very high standard. He used to laugh afterwards and say "What a load of rubbish!" Gradually he came to accept that something was happening over which he had no control.

As the weeks went by (we sat together once a week) he drifted into a trance state and a very guttural voice spoke to us. This turned out to be Ray's Austrian guide, who sounded very impatient as his English was limited at that time, but who now speaks perfectly.

The gentleman who is controlling Ray in writing this book is Sir Oliver Lodge, who when on earth was an eminent scientist, along with a group of other helpers from the Spirit World, or the Invisible World as he prefers to call it. He has given us some very profound lectures over the years and has been recorded by June on a number of tapes.

In our presence one evening, not long ago, Oliver Lodge asked June to place a new, empty audio tape into Ray's hand whilst

4

he was in trance. After a few minutes, this was put into a tape recorder and when June was told by our invisible friend to play it back, there were several minutes of Oliver Lodge's voice giving a lecture. When the tape finished, he concluded the lecture through Ray's voice whilst he was still in trance.

Whilst Ray is preparing to go into trance, June always plays a certain piece of music and one day we were told by Oliver Lodge that this piece of music would be temporarily erased. When we played the tape back, it was completely blank, but when we replayed it, it was restored. I asked how this was done and Oliver Lodge replied that it was by bending the sub-atomic electrons or impulses on the tape and then reversing the process to remove same. Not being scientifically or electronically educated, the foregoing may not be exact, but my wife and I will never forget this amazing experience.

Many people in the U.K., Spain and Gibraltar owe a lot to Ray and June for the effort they put into helping people in all sorts of situations. They organise meetings in Gibraltar, bringing out many excellent mediums from the U.K., with up to 400 people attending the meetings and they also use their home to hold seminars for the furtherance of Spiritual Knowledge and for healing that has helped many people, both physically and mentally.

Lately, Ray has broadcast on Spanish radio with Oliver Lodge (incidentally, he says he no longer wishes to be a Sir), doing a question and answer programme; many people responded by ringing to ask questions directly to Oliver Lodge and received immediate answers. The lady and gentleman announcers who conducted the programme were astounded at the results.

I could go on extolling the communication with the world of the Spirit, but it would take a book to do that.

God bless you, Ray and June, and may your work with Spirit go on ad infinitum and may closed scientific minds be opened by the words of Oliver Lodge.

MR. STEPHEN BARRY

On attending one of the trance sessions given by Mr. Raymond Smith, I had the opportunity to ask Oliver Lodge a question. I asked him to give me the meaning of C.R.B.D.S. Oliver said that he would do this as soon as the medium became conscious.

5

A short while after the meeting, Ray Smith gave me the words "Combe Rectory". This satisfied me that it was Oliver Lodge who was using the medium during his trance state.

I had obtained the information from the autobiography of Oliver Lodge, which stated that, when at school in Combe, he formed the Combe Rectory Birds Destruction Society.

MR. AND MRS. DAVIES

At a sitting with Ray and June Smith in Southern Spain, a neighbour's parrot, who had been squawking all afternoon, started exercising his vocal chords whilst Ray was in trance and Mentor was speaking. Mentor paused and said he would ask the parrot kindly to refrain from making a noise. Seconds later there was silence, which prevailed throughout the sitting.

We wish to thank Ray and June for the privilege of witnessing the phenomena of Oliver Lodge, Mesmer, Mentor and Phillippe through the trance mediumship of Ray.

MR. AND MRS. NAVARRO

When present at a trance sitting with Mr. Raymond Smith, my husband and I witnessed a voice being placed upon a virgin audio cassette. Oliver Lodge instructed the medium's wife to place the cassette between the hands of the medium. After about one minute, the cassette was placed in the player and the voice of Oliver Lodge said "Greetings", then gave the names of Abelardo, Victor, Mark and Eva. These were all names recognised by those present at that sitting.

Raymond Smith

PREFACE

Is physical death really the end of existence? Have my mother, father, relations and friends lived their lives for the meagre pleasures that life by chance seemed to offer them? I'm sure that many readers would agree that we all seem to spend much of our life struggling to provide ourselves and families with what we feel are necessities for our bodily comforts. Scientists suggest that our life began in the form of a virus, by the combination of certain chemicals and acids. By the process of evolution, survival of the fittest and preservation of species, here we are today still trying to fathom the purpose of our existence - if it has any. If life really did start in this way, I wonder why the scientists of today have not yet found the secret formula enabling them to be "Creators"? Even in early childhood, I found everything in visible existence so amazing that I yearned for an understanding of origin. It was important for me to try to understand how everything in life started and, even more, to understand what lies at the end of it all. I am told by my invisible friends that even within one single atom there is a law and order that the different particles seem to obey. If this be so, then surely it would be logical to ask what or who created this law and order, or did all the many elements of matter also form simply by chance? Perhaps as this book written by my inspirers gradually progresses, a little light may be thrown on this matter.

In the foreword of this book, I feel that I should try to explain why and how I came to be involved with hypnosis, to be followed in later years by trance mediumship.

I remember the time when I was four years old and would ask my parents "Will I go to heaven when I die?" It would seem that I was born wanting to know where I came from; even more importantly, where I would go when the end of my physical life came. If my parents assured me that I would go to heaven, then I slept well, but if for some reason they were too busy to reply, a cold sweat would break out on my forehead and a fear of death would prevent me from sleeping. My parents could not satisfy my insatiable desire for knowledge concerning both life and death. Like most young children in those days, I attended Sunday School, where it was impressed on my mind that God was a person who knew whether we did right or wrong. Stories about hell with its burning fires, punishments and terrible conditions were also told so that, instead of finding relief, my fear of death seemed to increase. After being a choir boy for a few years, promotion came when the vicar asked if I would like to become a server, assisting him in all the services that took place in church. This gave me an opportunity to draw close enough to the vicar so that I could ask him all those unanswered questions concerning death. In those days I honestly believed that the church was the house of God and that such people as the vicar were close enough to God as to know many of the secrets and mysteries of both life and death. "Tell me about life after death", I asked the vicar. What a disappointment for me when the only reply he could give was - "You just have to believe". Needless to say, my reign as a server soon came to a disappointing end. A relation of mine gave me a book entitled "My Philosophy", written by Sir Oliver Lodge, a gentleman of whom I had never heard. It captivated my interest so much that I read it many times trying to understand all the ideas postulated in its contents. About the same time, an aunty of mine gave me several small red books that were based upon the teachings, philosophy and phenomena embraced by Spiritualism. Within the pages of these books, especially "My Philosophy", I found many answers to those boyhood questions yet, for each question satisfactorily answered, many others would seem to come into my mind so that my task of trying to understand life and death grew bigger instead of smaller. I think this experience helped me to understand that one of the great purposes of life is learning - an eternal task. What a thought - to have to carry on learning for ever and ever!

My time spent doing National Service in the R.A.F. gave me another opportunity; that of attending religious services of various denominations, hoping once again that some rabbi, priest or chaplain would be able to help satisfy my thirst for knowledge in all these matters. It was not so, for I simply obtained a similar answer to that given me by the vicar - "You must believe". I admit that I am a biblical "doubting Thomas" and find it hard to just "believe". I need proof - "Show me the holes in your hands". I read "My Philosophy" once again, as well as other books written by intellectuals such as Arthur Findlay and Sir William Crookes and confess that they gave me much more comfort than I obtained from all those discussions that I had with church officials.

On completing my National Service, I attended Chester Diocesan Training College, so that I could become a schoolteacher. Every so often we had to go to schools to do what was called "teaching practice" and it was during one of these sessions that I met a very interesting teacher who practised hypnosis. My interest in this phenomenon was immediately aroused as this fellow teacher demonstrated the fascinating results that could be obtained by this phenomenon. This helped me to realise that there was a differentiation between mind and physical brain. It seemed to be a most useful key to help unlock some of those mysteries to do with both life and death. People even talked of living different lives; in other words reincarnation. If it was really true that we lived more than one life in this physical world, then we must have a soul, mind or spirit that went somewhere in between one life and another. That particular teacher taught me a lot concerning hypnosis and, ever since those days, I have learnt more and more. In fact, every time I use it as a tool to help someone I learn a little more, for no two patients are the same. Invisible friends often remind me that we are all as different as snowflakes, each having a different pattern. That, in itself, is to me a phenomenon.

Every Saturday morning we had to write one essay chosen from six that we had to prepare. To gain more experience in using hypnosis, I gathered together about five fellow students and, after putting them in a rather deep state of hypnosis, I would read to them notes concerning the essays that we had prepared and suggest to them that they would remember all the notes so that no matter which essay was chosen, all the relevant information was at hand within their minds. I also found that, by having to focus my mind on the notes, I also remembered the information, enabling me not to care which title of essay was chosen on Saturday mornings. In a sense this gave me my first practice of self-hypnosis for, apart from having a positive attitude to the matter in hand, self-hypnosis also involves the ability to put all other things to one side and behave rather like a horse wearing blinkers.

By this time I had married a charming young lady whom I met during my time in the Air Force. Her name was, or should I say still is, Mary. She was also interested in all psychic matters and we began to attend St. Helens Spiritualist Church, giving us an opportunity to witness the many visiting mediums. I can remember the elation in my mind after watching such mediums as Gordon Higginson demonstrate, but equally remember the disappointment after watching many others who were not as developed as Gordon. It was during this period that the church had an outing to Colwyn Bay to see a young medium demonstrate. His name was Ron Baker. We were so thrilled by his demonstration that I felt he should be part of the church at St. Helens. So it was that Ron came to live with my wife and me and, not surprisingly, became the president of the church. Apart from taking part in all church activities, Ron gave educational lectures involving the philosophy behind all spiritual knowledge and phenomena. I learned very much from listening to Ron as did the many who attended those lectures.

It was during those days that a Mrs. Yates, with her crystal ball, would visit groups of people in their homes and demonstrate her gift of clairvoyance with a difference. The phenomenon was unique because not only did Mrs. Yates see the visions, but the crystal could be passed from one guest to another for all would see the same. It is worth relating an incident that took place in my home. About eight or ten people attended that particular meeting, including an elderly lady by the name of Mrs. Bedworth. The medium could not understand the vision that she saw when talking to Mrs. Bedworth and when Mrs. Bedworth held the crystal, she said that what she saw resembled an animal. Another guest said that the vision was a tiger. As the crystal was passed around, I remarked that the tiger seemed to have human eyes. It was at this juncture that Mrs. Bedworth remembered that, in her days in South Africa when her husband was Consulate, servants used to dress up in animal skins to hold some sort of ceremony and that one particular servant would look exactly like the vision in the crystal. I understand that the medium, who in those days charged half a crown (2s.6d) had to give most of the money to her husband, who enjoyed more than one drink of Guinness. Many who still live in the area of Leigh will remember Mrs. Yates and her crystal.

My first witness of physical phenomena was when a friend took me to see a demonstration given by William Olsen. The medium was tied securely to a chair and also bound in a strait jacket. During the seance, his wife played music on an old gramophone, occasionally encouraging us to sing some well-known tunes. The trumpets flew all round the room then stopped near one of the visitors. A voice seemed to come from the trumpet and some of the guests claimed to recognise the voice. The climax of the evening came when the medium was projected in his chair through the air to the other side of the room. On landing, the strait jacket had been removed from his body. Since no voice spoke to me, I wondered whether it was just magic or whether it was truly a phenomenon of Spiritualism. In my ignorance in those days, I remember feeling that it seemed a pity that people who had died would engage themselves in a display of this nature. Since then, it has been explained to me by

12

my invisible friends that there are infinite levels of consciousness and that some of our friends in the Spirit World enjoy this sort of display.

A copy of Psychic News lies on my desk and in it I see letters discussing the validity of the materialisation medium Jimmy Gardner. I remember attending one of his seances in Wigan and must confess that, at that time, I was not very convinced, especially when one of his sitters told me that at some seances in the past even Jesus had materialised. This seemed too much for me to swallow. All this experience gave me a good grounding, so that today it does not surprise me that people who witness my trance sittings may think that the invisible friends who influence my mind are but other levels of my own personality. Many must question. Let us try to explain how this all started.

My work using hypnosis had continued all this time and I remember using it in some of the healing sessions held in St. Helens Spiritualist Church. In trying to help many people rid themselves of phobias and fears, I found that many would speak of previous lives in which some incident had occurred giving them this fear which, it seemed, they had brought with them into their present life. Remember that I was still attempting to answer those ever-expanding questions to do with birth, life and death, yet here comes another phenomenon with its accompanying questions - Reincarnation.

Have we all lived more than this present life and, if so, how many lives have we lived? Do animals and other kingdoms of life reincarnate and how does this affect the theory of rebirth? At what stage in the evolution of mind or soul does the self retain individuality? Such questions as these arose in my mind, adding to the confusion that had been caused by all those previous unanswered enquiries.

At the early age of 33, my wife became ill with a tumour on her brain, this coinciding with a visit to the church of Fanny Higginson, Gordon's mother. I took a lock of my wife's hair to a private sitting at which I was told that my wife would pass that year as the leaves fell. Fanny told me that the lady who was helping me to nurse my wife would eventually marry me. "You won't be able to have any more children", said Fanny. The lady in question did marry me and every fact given to me in that memorable sitting has since come true. There did seem to be a plan behind all the events that took place for my new companion in life had the same avid interest in all these matters as myself. She persuaded me to give up my

13

yacht in which we sailed with our collective four children for nine years.

I must give credit to the inspiration of my wife June, or maybe I should say her inspirers, for the days spent sailing to different countries gave me a respect of nature - the mother part of God, that I did not have before this adventure. It would require a separate book to relate the many incidents that befell the family in those nine years spent visiting many ports and countries.

This preface resembles an autobiography yet I feel it is important to relate how the trance state first manifested and how it seems that all the many previous chapters of my life seemed to be a preparation for the chapters that I am now living and no doubt for those to follow - God willing.

After those nine years at sea passed, we sold the yacht in Gibraltar. By then the children had reached that stage in life when they wanted to have their own companions, so they stayed in Gibraltar whilst June and I returned to England for a short period.

June told me that, even as a young girl, she would often hear her name being called by some invisible friend and would many times look round, finding no-one there. She was, and is, obviously clairaudient, as is her daughter Annette. I remember that Annette would often ask my youngest son Mark to sleep in her room because she would often see spirit friends, not understanding at that time what was taking place. Mark tells me that he spent many nights sleeping in a chair so that Annette could sleep in peace.

Mediumship does seem to be hereditary, for my granddaughter is also plagued, or should I say blessed, with the same sensitivity as her mother. To continue:

One night my wife June woke me up in the middle of the night telling me that during my sleep I had been speaking German. The communicator told her not to be afraid, as he was around us to help and guide us. We used to have meetings with some of our mediumship friends who, at the end of every session, would describe that of which they had become aware. When my turn came, I had to admit that I had received very little compared with the many visions of colour and even personalities that they had received. Then, on a much later occasion, I seemed to go off into a deep sleep. On awakening, my friends told me that I had been in a trance state and that Mentor had communicated to them. Due to my keen interest and work involving hypnosis, I felt that the reason for this must have been the fact that some hidden desire of mine wanted to manifest, taking on the assumed personality of such a well-known and historical figure. When I listen to the recordings of those earlier days, there is no comparison with that which transpires now.

We are here to learn from our mistakes and I am still learning. At one seminar to which I was invited to talk on and demonstrate hypnosis I, in my ignorance of what was happening to me, agreed to sit for trance before about sixty people. One person at that meeting asked if the trance could be done in German, since that was the language of my inspirer. It was explained that, since my brain pattern or brain computer was programmed in English with a little French, the communication would have to be conducted in those languages. I'm afraid, because of the lady's insistence, that particular session gave me my first lesson. To some is given the gift of speaking in tongues and that gift was not given to me. My first trance demonstration disappointed me so much that, on returning home, I vowed to myself that further sittings would only take place within the protection of my own home.

As this gift gradually developed, other personalities seemed to manifest. Were these even other fractions of my deep inner self expressing themselves by taking on the guise of such people? Who was this person called Phillippe who said that, when living, he was the Marquis de Peysegur and of the Chasenet family? Since that time, he has proved to be a great philosopher and, at the same time, a personality capable of lifting the vibrations from a serious to a jovial nature.

Then came a guest speaker - Sir Oliver Lodge - who now is a guest no longer; he seems to have taken up permanent residence somewhere in my mind. He apparently died when I was ten years old and, apart from obtaining his book "My Philosophy" so many years ago, I had no idea that he had spent so much time researching mediums, together with various phenomena embraced within Spiritualism. He, with the help of other invisible friends, have so far expressed their thoughts on nearly a thousand hours of recorded trance sessions. He has agreed to express many of those thoughts in the chapters that follow in this book.

Others who have manifested include Sister Mary, my own father and one they call the great light - Mentor. When asked about his life and name, Mentor has said "Which life and name would you have me speak of? I am what I am as a result of my total evolution through all God's Kingdoms".

In my hypnosis sessions of the past, I used to plan according to the problem that people would feel they had. Now when I am privileged to help people using hypnosis as a tool, words seem to be placed in my mouth, making the task much easier.

So many facts have been given to me by my invisible friends concerning their personal lives and interests that I must now conclude that the information given at least comes from some external source. I know that I have never read them in any books nor heard of them from any other source. Naturally, my wife and I have checked that they are true and, in so doing, have discovered many interesting points. We all seem to have the same interests in life - Science, Mathematics, Astronomy, Sport, Music and many others. Maybe this contributes towards the fact that our minds seem to vibrate on the same or similar frequency. I remember well one occasion when I sat for some friends down here in Spain. I am sure they will not object if I mention their names. Micky and Tracey met us in a restaurant and, during the meal, we talked of hypnosis and trance. They had never been involved in any psychic matters, but seemed so interested that on the same evening I regressed Tracey enabling her to become aware of at least one previous life. Their interest was so much aroused that they asked if they could witness a trance session. The following day they had to make a journey near to Austria. In talking to Franz, Micky asked him to give facts relative to where he was buried. They were told about a certain church and churchyard in Meersburg, where they would find Mesmer's triangular tomb with engravings on the three sides, one of which was of our solar system with its various planets. When they returned, they brought with them photographs to verify that all information given was correct. Micky also told of how their hair seemed to stand up as they left that particular churchyard containing the tomb of Franz Anton Mesmer. If you knew Micky, you would know that he was not one to have his hair raised, no matter what befell him. Just one small piece of evidence - many more to follow. As Oliver would say, no one piece of evidence is sufficient to convince mankind of the survival of human personality, but only a conglomeration of many.

Looking back, (incidentally the title of one of Arthur Findlay's books), it seems that there may well be a plan behind all our lives and that we came back with some deep-seated knowledge of this plan. The plan obviously allows us to use our free will so that, from all the painful mistakes we make in our life, the purpose of our return here gradually comes into focus. For myself, it seems that the years spent teaching mathematics and other subjects has enabled me to appear before many people with reasonable confidence, so that I may share with them the thoughts that are transmitted to my mind. The link with June and our work together enabled me to retire at an early age, thus giving me an opportunity for greater research into modern phenomena.

One of the common interests that I share with both invisible and earthly friends is music. At the age of eleven, I learned to play the cornet. This enabled me to have the experience of playing with several brass bands and being subject to discipline. It was indeed this common interest that brought June and I together. Once again, a book could be devoted to how music has played such an important role not only in my own life, but the lives of all the family, who have performed together many times on both television and radio. Whenever I now sit for trance or meditate, the music that we play seems to facilitate my drifting away rather quickly, so that my mind does not interfere with the telepathic reception of external influences. No doubt, when eventually I put myself entirely to one side, my friends will tell you that in some of those higher spheres, music, art and other creative forces even replace language. We now hold intercourse daily with our friends on the other side and, because of this, it was suggested that we share those thoughts with you. The main reason why it has been necessary to write this introduction is to show how and why it came to me that this union has transpired.

Now we live in a large villa here in Spain and use it as the Gibraltar Psychic Research Centre. We have many meetings and invite the better-known mediums from England to demonstrate their gifts in a large theatre in Gibraltar. June works daily using her lovely gift of healing and I still practice my hypnosis, using it as a tool to help people, even to develop their psychic gifts. Seminars are held here when groups of people come, mainly from England, and spend a week with us. This gives us an opportunity to share with others that which we have and to gain from them that which we have not. We research into all the phenomena of Spiritualism and also try to keep up to date by investigating what could be called modern phenomena.

Only recently, part of our society went to a small village in Spain where a rather strange phenomenon occurs. There, faces manifest in the concrete floor of a house occupied by an old lady. These faces constantly change and, so far, no satisfactory explanation has been found.

Many readers must be familiar with Raymond Moody's book "Life after Life", based on his research with people who have neared death, hence called "the near death experience". Instead of believing all that is written in such books, we do our own investigation by interviewing people who claim to have temporarily died. Out of the many interesting interviews I have had, one particular case is worth relating. Only a few months ago, I took Sveno, a Danish man, with me to a radio station in Marbella. Sveno told how, during the last war, he helped to get Jews out of Denmark. Unfortunately, he was caught, interned, tortured, beaten and suffered a near death experience. During his temporary death, he left his body, went through the usual experiences, eventually able to see his own home in Denmark. All the furniture had been moved and a sculpture that he had completed was in pieces. He had told his wife to keep it moist so that it would not crack. When he astrally entered his bedroom, he saw his wife in bed with another man. On release from the concentration camp, he was able to verify that all that he had seen in his O.O.B.E. had taken place. Needless to say, he divorced his wife and later on married again. Certainly, experiences similar to this seem to prove that, in certain circumstances, something exteriorises from the physical body. Whether it survives after physical death or not is one of the mysteries that we are all trying to solve. Evidence from other phenomena within Spiritualism - materialisation, direct voice, psychic photography and much more does seem to suggest that human personality does survive physical death.

I have been privileged to be invited several times to work in Stansted Hall and other venues, where Spiritualists have gathered together with the better-known mediums. At such gatherings, lectures on numerology, astrology, yoga, healing and many other topics are given by invited speakers. Mediums demonstrate their gifts and talk on the development of mediumship, as well as give private sittings. Some may disagree as I make the following comment, but this is the truth as I see it. Demonstrations of mediumship, together with private sittings, seem to be the most popular, as people quite naturally have a desire to link with relations and friends who have already journeyed from earthly dimensions to those of a higher vibration. Many may be fortunate, feeling that the information given by mediums has been sufficient for them to feel that those who communicate really do still live in an invisible world - invisible in relation to matter. For myself, I still question as to why the invisible friends only seem to give snippets of information instead of a string of personal details that would leave no doubt in our minds.

Many who have preceded us have left coded messages and

Many who have preceded us have left coded messages and promised to impinge their thoughts on the mind of a suitable channel so that the messages could be deciphered. Frederick Myers and Oliver Lodge number amongst many who left such coded messages in an effort to convince those of us still living that there was life after physical death. Why is this? Even my own mother promised to try her best to return with irrefutable evidence of her survival yet, so far, in my opinion, she has not achieved this.

There are so many questions to be answered. Perhaps this is the reason why Oliver Lodge suggested to my wife that an appropriate title for his book, written from the invisible world, could be "Nobody Wants To Listen - And Yet". Answers to my infinite number of enquiries have already been given by those who seem to use me as a channel. Let us hope, as we sift through the many recordings of trance, that answers to this and many other questions will be satisfactorily answered, that you, as readers, may want to listen and, having listened, will still say..."and yet".

As I conclude the preface of this book, a microphone has been placed near to my chair so that the opening chapter may be recorded on this very day. Parts of this book will contain information already received in past trance sittings and others will, no doubt, be added as we continue to link with thoughts transmitted through the ether by those capable of vibrating the essence of my mind. Prove to Oliver Lodge and friends that there are some minds willing to listen. In the future you and I may have the opportunity of reaching their minds with further questions as we say to them "And Yet".

NOBODY WANTS TO LISTEN - AND YET.

Now is the time for this book to start
Our joy and pleasure the veil to part
Blending our thoughts with yours to try
Obtain answers to wherefore and why
Do not expect us all mysteries to solve
Yet our prayers that your fears will dissolve
With my friends assembled here
All I assure you so very sincere
Never will we your mind deceive
Truth will replace all you believe
So share with all you count as a friend
The joy that life has truly no end
Of this we here are all very sure
Love is eternal and ever so pure
I pray this communion to you gives some pleasure
So you may gain some of God's treasure
That he gives so freely to all in earth's school
Enjoy his gift - be not the fool
No end to learning is there ever
And when death that cord doth sever
Nothing will cease your endless climb
Dwelling in spheres without any time
Yesterday's worries will instantly end
Enabling you to forever send
Truth to all others - your sisters and brothers.

Communication

Chapter 1

COMMUNICATION

From the world of the mind - greetings. You may wonder why this chapter started with a combined poem and acrostic, yet those of you familiar with one of my books - "Raymond" - will know that often my son would write to us in similar style. It was his only means of informing us of his whereabouts during his short time spent fighting for his country.

Many here in different levels of consciousness take what opportunities there are to express their reflections on life and rebirth. It is because communication comes from so many levels of mind that, often, there may seem to be conflicts of opinion. However, allow me first to express my gratitude for the opportunity to use this channel, so that I may put right some of the opinions I expressed in the many books I wrote concerning the survival of human personality and all its implications.

Only when you understand more of the conditions that prevail after physical death will you be able to appreciate the difficulties in transmitting thoughts from our mind world to your physical world. This is one reason why I chose the title "Nobody wants to listen - and yet". It is not sufficient to try to link with your relatives and friends in our world. The more you understand how mind really works, the less likely you are to need further incarnations of a physical nature; in other words, the more likely you are to be able to enter those higher mental and majestic spheres, the description of which is beyond earthly words.

I wonder that anyone read the books that I wrote as, on reflection, I realise more than ever that science is based upon observations made through the five physical senses. It falls far short in its ability to apply itself to an understanding of telepathy and senses that lie outside physical perception. There is a great difference between education, intelligence and spirituality. I feel that, in writing many of those books, I utilised my education in a rather unintellectual manner, for I even used a dictionary so that I might impress readers into believing my vocabulary was extensive. This action was without intelligence and certainly unspiritual. Let me, as I continue, try to rectify this by expressing my thoughts in a more simplistic style. To those of you who may have read some of those books, I ask your forgiveness. The more limited vocabulary of this channel we are privileged to use may therefore prove to be a great asset.

Why have we waited until now to express these thoughts through this and other channels? Like fruit in the garden that tastes better when it has fully ripened, in the same way, we in invisible dimensions must seek, wait and find a mind that vibrates on a similar frequency to ours. No two minds are identical, just as the pattern of each snowflake differs. However, it is just possible, sometimes, to find two snowflakes with very similar patterns so that, through a microscope, if placed on top of one another, they would appear to be in reasonable symmetry.

The group of which I am part finds that one or two channels are capable of changing our thoughts into words without too much interference. A radio station can only be heard well if the transmitter and receiver are on the same frequency, the transmitter is powerful and there is little interference from other stations. Like many in the living and invisible world, the minds of the inhabitants are often filled with thoughts of a gross, material and physical nature. Like attracts like. We have had to wait until that physical and material cloud cleared away from this channel, so that clairaudient transmissions could be heard. Naturally, the occasional cloud and storm pass over this receiver, then thoughts become a little distorted. In writing this script, should this occur, we will wait for a clearing of the mind or the clearing of material thoughts, before continuing transmissions.

A baby developing in its mother's womb is connected through the umbilical cord to the physical lining of that womb. By this means, the requirements for physical development are transmitted through that cord until nature determines the time of birth, when the cord is severed. No language is necessary during this process. A parallel may be observed by us in the fact that the mind is connected by a similar silver cord to the etheric double, a semi-physical energy field that, in turn, affects the physical body. Once again, no language is necessary for one to affect the other. I mention this in endeavouring to explain that, in clairaudience and trance, no physical language can be utilised. A thought is transmitted from our minds to parts of the mind of this instrument so that the etheric may receive it. From then onwards, it is a natural process for that thought to be expressed in words, depending upon the level of consciousness of the medium. I am trying to stress the fact that thought needs no language.

Here in our dimensions, free of physical limitations, we communicate by thought. Those in levels nearer to earth may feel that they are speaking in a similar fashion to when they were living, they are simply linking mind to mind. In other words, once free of the physical body, that process known as extra sensory perception works to a much higher degree of perfection. Not only information and memories may be passed from one mind to another, but even emotions and mannerisms of the communicator.

For us to convey to you the truth as we know it, we require that the higher mind of this medium should not transmit at the same time, otherwise that truth may be distorted. The process of communication is quite complex and requires much explanation, since it is not only limited to clairaudience, clairvoyance and clairsentience, but is also involved in all other known mental and physical phenomena. Spiritualists tend to think that communication is from discarnate to incarnate. Not at all. It is possible for the incarnate to communicate mind to mind, this process proved by my friend Frederick Myers. I admit that the physical does interfere and that, whenever mind is chained to physical conditions, transmission of thought is limited. Mind can also influence matter by a process of slowing the rate of vibration, demonstrated by some rather unique individuals and called telekinesis. This effect may be achieved by the minds in either visible or invisible dimensions; I therefore feel my comment about Spiritualists is quite justified, for they tend to think that all physical phenomena is the result of influence from our worlds. It is difficult to decide whether the intelligence controlling such phenomena originates from the minds of the "living" or the "dead". Only careful research and sifting of the information received can help decide this, in both physical and mental phenomena. I am reminded of a comment I made that is often quoted - and I am still of the same opinion - "No single observation can prove the survival of human personality, but only a continuous collection of evidence from all available phenomena". Crookes, Myers, Richet, myself and other friends were only able to conclude survival by the observation of all phenomena available in our days.

We, in these levels of consciousness, are aware of modern developments in your technology. Because of this, many groups in our level try to influence the particles of iron oxide on your magnetic tapes, just as, in days of old, light-sensitive paper was used in photography. Spirit photography, direct voice, materialisation, transfiguration and other phenomena have not convinced mankind of the reality of survival. I doubt very much whether any influences, mental or physical, will achieve this aim except to those whose minds are sufficiently open. One day the pendulum of man's interests will swing from the materialistic to a more spiritual outlook. In the meantime, we here try to prepare for that time by using whatever channels are available; it is our chosen task to plant seeds of knowledge in the minds of those whose mental ground is fertile, so that when the wind of change blows, those seeds will find their way to greater fields.

Many who consult sensitives do so in the hope that some idea of what lies ahead in their physical life may be given by inhabitants of our worlds. With regard to prediction, I have often tried to suggest that life in both visible and invisible worlds is full of twists and turns. It is natural to want to know what lies around the next corner yet, if we knew, we may not want to go around that corner. All learning is, in a way, painful for it expands or stretches the mind. This can only be achieved by experiences, some of which are, at the time, unpleasant. This law not only applies to the world of matter, but also to the mind world; our world. The advice given to us by those in higher levels of mind is to accept that whatever lies around the twists and turns of infinite progression is a necessary challenge. By overcoming challenges, we add experience to knowledge, thus becoming wiser. Wisdom is one of the necessary tools that we may use to grow spiritually rich and enable us to move forward along that never-ending spiritual pathway.

When we can communicate with you, there are natural laws that limit our transmissions, thus ensuring that you strive for knowledge. Do not expect information to be served like a tasty meal to you, but ask your invisible friends to help raise the level of your mind. We can only understand that which our minds are capable of comprehending. Only when the mind is thirsty can your friends offer you that nectar of the Gods. I therefore implore all those who wish to feed spiritual comfort to their fellow man to ask and continue asking; you will receive if the time is right. Remember, not everyone is endowed with the gift of discernment of spirit. You have the gift that your mind needs - not what it wants. Your friends in invisible dimensions can only feed to you that which they know is necessary for your progress and this often differs from your wants.

We are aware that you now have more evidence of the other self than we ever had. The number of individuals who experienced either being out of the body, or what you call near death experience, was no doubt less than prevails today. Modern techniques in resuscitation obviously enable people to survive heart attacks, accidents and other physical torments of life. It was a more rare experience to meet such individuals in my day. Those who had these experiences

26

refrained from talking about them in case they were classified as insane, whereas now conversation about such topics is quite common. The list of phenomena suggesting the reality of the existence of a dual "you" grows bigger each decade, yet the pendulum still seems to pause nearer to the material side of its swing than the spiritual.

Still, in connection with communication from our realm to yours, I ask you to pause and consider some of those instances when, due to accident or whatever, individuals find themselves away from their physical bodies. Through this channel I am aware of the experiences many of them would relate. Imagine then, that some wonderful medium could communicate with such an exteriorised mind, be able to see that soul clairvoyantly and clairaudiently and be able to hear their thoughts. Do you feel that through this communication the medium could receive from them answers to the mysteries and secrets of creation? Much more likely that the poor soul outside of his body would ask the medium what had happened. From this example you may see that communication with those on earth may be easier before ascending that tunnel into the light of one's new level of consciousness, yet very limited as regards the information that may be received. On physical death, most minds that, for a while, stay close to earthly vibrations are in a rather confused state, although very often capable of affecting earthly objects. It is common knowledge that, within a very short period of death, clocks seem to stop and other similar strange occurrences take place. However, I do assure you that having arrived in that level of mind appropriate to one's moral and spiritual values (Spirituality), then communication with those left on earth is not so easy.

Let me once again use the principles involved in transmission and reception of radio waves to draw another parallel. If the transmitter is very near to the receiver, then audio signals can be received even if the two frequencies vary slightly. As the transmitter and receiver move further away from each other, several factors must be considered to ensure even moderate reception. These factors include the power of the transmitter, the type and efficiency of the receiving antenna, the type of transmission or narrowness of wave band and the actual frequency used, as well as other considerations. I did promise to give simple explanations, but feel that this is a most useful comparison. In other words, as one ascends in invisible levels of consciousness, the conditions necessary for reception of transmitted thoughts become much more complex. Just as sensitives on earth would band together, so increasing the effectiveness of healing energies, so we assembled in our group work together to increase the transmission power of thought. As mentioned earlier, we also have to find an earthly sensitive who can receive our mental frequency. Even so, transmissions often become distorted by interference from other transmissions, as well as certain higher atmospheric conditions.

To receive thought from higher levels or higher minds, it obviously needs a living sensitive whose mind is capable of "tuning in" to those higher frequencies of mind. Is it any wonder, then, that communication through earthly sensitives is not always as one would desire? It is a little like trying to hear the voice of someone using a megaphone three hundred yards away when a strong wind is blowing. In these circumstances, one would hear only sections of what the megaphonist was shouting. Often, then, thoughts from those on our side of the veil seem to be disjointed and even insignificant, because the main substance of thought transmission has been blown away by "earthly wind". It was often like this when I had the opportunity of 'sitting' with Mrs. Piper, Mrs. Leonard and other similar good mediums of my day. Sometimes I felt exhilarated and, at other times, so disappointed that doubt of continued existence would swell up in my mind, making me feel that, maybe, some of my more sceptical friends were correct in their alternative hypothesis to survival. Here, allow me to stand to one side, so that a greater light in our group may add thoughts with regard to communication. Those with whom we communicate call this light "Mentor".

"Physical life on this speck of dust within God's creation is rather like that of the caterpillar on the leaf of the cabbage. In that incarnated form, the caterpillar may feel that the leaf is its world. It struggles in taking steps to avoid other forms of life devouring it and tries, whilst so doing, to both eat and shelter from the elements of nature. In a similar fashion, man thinks that the planet earth offers all that can be expected from life. Earth is his cabbage leaf.

"Most people are aware that, eventually, at the end of caterpillar life, comes the chrysalis stage when the body is enveloped by a cocoon. To the casual observer, the caterpillar seems dead, but with patience the observer would see the life force adorn itself with that beautiful body of the butterfly, now able to leave that mundane world of the cabbage leaf. This life force now finds itself in a new world of which it had no previous memory or even anticipation. The butterfly flies off, discovering that the world is much bigger than the confinement of its birthplace. So you see that man, at the end of his physical 'caterpillar' life, would also seem to die and be cocooned. To those sensitive to perceive comes the vision that man also emerges from the physical, adorning himself with an etheric garment and finds himself free of the physical confinements of time, distance, speed, past, present and future. In this new environment, he may not even want to remember the restrictions of earth and finds that opportunities that he could not even dream of now present themselves. Love does persist. Those who have preceded you into that great freedom, know that 'in no time' you too will pass through that same chrysalis stage to find and join them in a world beyond the description of earthly words. The butterfly may find it difficult to communicate with the caterpillar it left behind, yet still holds love thoughts and memories within its small soul.

"May I, in passing this thought, thank you for the opportunity of trying to be of service, one of the greatest qualities in the enhancement of the greatest of all - Love. Thank you."

Well now, maybe you see a little more clearly the reasons why your friends, living in these infinite levels of consciousness, find it hard to convey their thoughts, memories and feelings to those they have left behind. I do pray that the explanations concerning difficulties of communication are more easily understood given in this manner, rather than in the laborious attempts made in the latter section of my book "Raymond". You may wonder whether the fact that the earthly name of this channel is Raymond is purely coincidental with the fact that the name of one of my six sons is Raymond. Is there, indeed, any such thing as coincidence?

Communication mind to mind is not a simple topic to discuss with you. As previously mentioned, you may link telepathically with one another or we may try to link with you. Just as your physical body handicaps transmissions from our world to yours so, in a similar way, the etheric body restricts the reception of thoughts given to us from those who have cast off their etheric garment. We may only receive thoughts with clarity from those in the next highest dimension. Similarly, those who exist in very low levels would not understand our transmissions. Remember, the link between levels of mind is achieved by what you call telepathy.

With regard to communications such as this, I am reminded of a statement I made concerning the evidence I received from my friend Myers, through such mediums as Mrs. Piper, Mrs. Leonard, Mrs. Verral and others. I felt that Myers' personality and thoughts differed slightly with each medium, no doubt due to the fact that they were diluted by the various channels used. However, in each case, sufficient information was given to leave me in no doubt that it was my friend trying telepathically to convey his thoughts to me. In the case of those sensitives who were in deep unconscious trance, this dilution was less noticeable.

Imagine that you and a friend feel that you are reasonably capable of communicating mind to mind. The person transmitting may try to send a thought encouraging the receiver to say "put the kettle on", but the receiver may utter the words "a cup of tea". The thought is essentially the same, but the method of expressing it is different. Thus it is that the 'language of thought' is different from earthly words. This may help to explain why my sealed packet containing seven envelopes, one inside the other, did not provide evidence of my survival as I had hoped and planned. One sensitive became aware that there was a reference to music; another, I feel, obtained a number five and others obtained part of the contents. In actual fact, the main statement of the contents referred to my habit of practising the five finger piano exercise on my writing desk. My friend Myers had the same difficulty in trying to communicate with me in what is now known as "The Famous Message". Why didn't my friend tell me of the imminent death of my son Raymond, instead of disguising it by using part of the "Horatio" passage in literature? I feel the explanation given above about trying to send a thought suffices.

I hope by now you can see that several factors limit the transmission of words through sensitives. To summarise. It is thought that we try to send from our world to yours and not language. That thought may be diluted by the mind of the medium. The chance that the correct name or words used by the medium in relaying that thought is very small. When the medium in question is in an unconscious state of trance, there is more chance of exact words being received.

Vibrations through the ether of space need some form of matter to make us aware of their existence. Light, heat, magnetism, gravity and cohesion all need some form of matter upon which they can act before we can sense their presence. In the same way, higher vibrations of thought need something physical before you can receive them. Radio waves need a wireless receiver, whereas we need a medium. It has taken approximately thirty years of work before this channel (Raymond) became a suitable receiver for our thoughts. By changing vibrations within the ether, we may direct energy so that it affects either the mind of the sensitive or even physical objects; mental and physical phenomena. A full chapter could be devoted to each of these, but it is my desire to speak about those matters that I feel even more important, such as the conditions that prevail in these infinite levels of mind, other kingdoms of life, prayer and the many questions that this channel directs towards us. You will remember that I stressed the importance of asking before you receive. Because of this, we may only give our thoughts on the many questions that this sensitive sends in our direction. Let me mention some of those that have perplexed his mind in recent months and then, in later chapters, try to give some satisfactory answers to them.

When Siamese twins are born, are there two souls? Why should such things occur? Do animals survive and, if so, where? Are there animals, birds, insects, rivers, seas, etc. in our world? Where is our world? Is there a finite end to the evolution and progression of spirit? Is it against God's law to transplant human organs? There is no end to the asking of questions by this sensitive and, for every satisfactory answer accepted, he seems to find at least another ten questions. Our task is infinite. We too ask questions and find ourselves in the same dilemma. Just as you can seek and find experts in earthly matters, we also, in similar manner can ask those who have greater experience in spiritual matters.

From the previous paragraphs, you will see that communication truly has its limitations, especially from the mind world to those still attached to their earthly physical bodies. Let us, therefore, move on to discuss other matters, in the hope that some of the ideas postulated may enable you to conclude that the progression of mind is infinite.

The Butterfly World

Chapter 2

THE BUTTERFLY WORLD

If the butterfly could communicate with its offspring the caterpillar, no doubt the caterpillar would find it hard to understand the descriptions given; imagine trying to describe your human experiences to a fish swimming in the ocean. It is a similar task that I undertake in this chapter. There are many types of butterflies living in different parts of your planet and, hence, the story of each would differ. In the same way, I can only relate the environment in which I and my friends exist, apart from other levels that I have been shown.

You will notice that often I refer to my friends in the group here, all of whom are of similar mind. A question that I often feel through etheric wavelengths is "Where is your wife and family, are they with you?" Just as in earthly life one tried to work and play with others of like mind, finding oneself linking with several groups of people, so life in my world is spent working with different groups. Atoms combine to form molecules. Molecules combine to form cells or whatever. This gregarious law seems to apply in both earthly and invisible worlds. As individual atoms of mind, we group together to form a molecule of mind. That in turn forms part of a bigger unit and each unit part of the whole of that level of consciousness. When I look back into my earthly experiences, I see that not all of my family were of the same level of mind as myself. Their mental and spiritual specific gravity was different. Shortly after the severance of that silver umbilical cord, the mind gravitates to its own level, similar to the process involved in the fractional distillation of crude oil into lighter oils; paraffin, petroleum and other products. The petroleum is not aware of other products in this process. Each unit is only aware of its immediate neighbours and that it is part of a whole. This seems rather a poor parallel but the only one that comes to mind. In the initial stages of this process, materials of different specific gravities are together until they find their suitable level. One may take oil to the bottom of the river, but it will find its way to the surface. In the same way we may travel to lower levels of consciousness but, having completed our task, rise once again to our own level. There is one big problem with this analogy even though it contains some similarities. It is an earthly process devoid of emotion, intuition and those finer vibrations of love. Because of love, after physical death one is met by a host of souls, some who had been relations or friends during earthly life and others who seem just as familiar.

Even in earthly life, I remember dreaming. In some of those dreams I would be with people who seemed just as important to me as any relations or friends on earth. For some of them I felt great affection. I realise now that amongst the host that met me on my rebirth, were souls with whom I had shared experiences in the evolution of my mind. To answer that question: Yes, my wife, family and close friends numbered amongst that host of dear souls welcoming me to the butterfly world. Then that fractional distillation of mind gradually took place and, after that, a magnetic, empathetic love attraction to those whose company I am privileged to share in this and other groups. When thoughts of love are received from my wife, family and friends in other levels, I find that just by a thought I am with them in whatever environment is befitting to us. By the creative ability of our minds, my wife and I can meet in an etheric double of Mariemont, an earthly house in which we shared both the joys and problems of life. Everything that exists in any level of consciousness does so only by the creative ability of the minds of its inhabitants. We share one another's creations and, on arrival, add to them by the experiences we have brought with us.

If this statement be true, then those minds who appreciate the music Mozart and other similar great musicians wrote, may either listen to such music or, if one has the experience of playing a musical instrument, play it in the orchestra. Likewise, those who would like to learn to play an instrument in that same orchestra will find no shortage of teachers. All this and more without the necessity of earthly limitations such as money, time and handicaps, physical or mental. Because of the sum creation of all, in my level of mind there are all the things that I enjoyed in my earthly existence and still find necessary, including universities, libraries, laboratories and facilities for various sports. Naturally, others in the same mind world create and share their interests, so we have all the beauties of nature and art. There are landscapes with colours so intense that no earthly words would describe them. Some of my friends enjoy those activities or interests associated with water - we have brooks, streams, rivers and seas.

I realise that, if I continue in this vein, I would give the impression that everything here in my world is in a state of perfection - to you it may sound like Utopia or Nirvana. Not so. We learn from those in higher states of mind that progress can only be made by being of service to others. I therefore spend much time sharing my scientific thoughts with others on my level, as well as visiting other lower levels trying to help those souls reach for a higher level of understanding. In the same manner, we are privileged to listen to the thoughts expressed by minds whose luminosity is far brighter than ours. Sometimes we are taken by our teachers to that level in which they dwell, as in the same way we bring those in lower levels of consciousness to see our world. Only those who are desirous of reaching higher are taken on such journeys.

I have mentioned some of the conditions that prevail in our mind world, the level that we, as a group, find ourselves. Those who live in those lower levels of mind do not appreciate the same things as we do and, therefore, in those levels, universities, libraries and laboratories do not exist. A memory comes to mind of a communication I had from my son Raymond, through the mediumship of Mrs. Piper. He told me that he could have a whisky and soda. In that level in which he first found himself, he could partake of such things because, in those first stages of his rebirth, that was his desire. If one desires to pursue such earthly activities one may do so, until the realisation comes that the mind has no need of them. In lower levels still, the inhabitants still desire the same sordid attractions in which they involved themselves when attached to their earthly body. Some of the groups to whom we try to communicate through this channel would sometimes ask whether sexual relationships exist in the "spirit world". I reiterate; there is not one "spirit world", but an infinite number of levels of consciousness and certainly in some, if it be their wish, those in that level may involve themselves in such low levels of expressing desire. Let me take this opportunity of saying that such earthly pleasures bear no comparison with the ability to merge one's mind with another's. This total merging of any two souls cannot be compared with the partial penetration involved in, what on earth, is most inaptly called "making love". As we rise through these levels of mind, the meaning of love becomes more profound. None that I know have any conception of what is meant by divine love.

Questions with regard to our worlds constantly reach us from the mind of this sensitive, such as: In your world are there countries, cities, towns, animals, birds, insects, trees, flowers and cigarettes? The last because he smokes, as did I. Allow me then to take this opportunity to try to throw some light on these matters, so that he also may feel some satisfaction in the thoughts we now express.

First, with regard to countries, cities and towns. Remember

that you gravitate to that level which suits your mind and its desires. Those who would be happier in the city naturally find themselves in such an environment, with all the attractions that the city can offer. Are not some of you in earthly conditions more happy in the city than in the country? Would you be happy to find yourself in the middle of the Sahara Desert? Those who have chosen to help you in your transition from the physical world to the mind world know what surroundings would occasion less shock as you emerge into your level. No doubt some nomads would be happier to find themselves in a desert rather than a city. This initial panorama does not persist indefinitely. As you progress spiritually, you find yourself in the environment which best suits your state of mind. During the war, many of Dowding's young pilot friends found themselves in planes, still fighting the enemy, for those were the conditions of their minds at the time of physical death. There are always friends whose chosen task it is to help you realise that you are no longer in the physical world. As this realisation gradually, or instantly, takes place, depending on the beliefs of the individual, the mind becomes aware that these initial conditions are no longer necessary. Some refuse even to accept that they have died, and find themselves in a confused state still in earthly dimensions, earthbound. What is paradise for one may be hell for another. Not every soul enjoys the music of the masters.

In the same way, your invisible friends know whether it would be more apt for you to "wake up" in England, Africa, China or wherever. They know exactly who should be there amongst the host of welcoming friends. As you progress through these levels, your mental horizon broadens and, as it does, you learn to be just as content in any section of the sphere in which you find yourself. Colours of etheric skin, different cultures and interests all seem to blend much more than they ever did when you had earthly skin.

Amongst that welcoming host are not only your earthly human friends, but also those animal and bird friends to whom you gave love and affection, thus enabling them to retain their individuality for as long as necessary. Reincarnation is not only a subject involving the human species but even all other kingdoms, including the mineral, but I will make comment on this later. As a family, we had many animal and bird friends, among them a peacock we named "Mr. Jackson". He was there, together with some of my pigeons and also Curly, Larry, Vix and Bob and others of the dog level of mind. Only now do I begin to understand how this could be so. You will remember I stressed that here we exist in groups, no matter what

36

sphere or level we live in. To give this some meaning, let us take one level in one sphere as an example.

It is possible that, in that one level of mind, there would be some who had a dislike of insects, whereas others in the same level may be happy surrounded by such creatures. Even in the same level of mind, groups join together according to the mutual desires and interest of that group. Sensitives often relate that, in a vision, they have become aware that in the invisible world there are trees, flowers, birds, fish and similar conditions to those experienced on earth. This is so and, yet, even more. The creative and imaginative ability of mind enables that mind to create forms that did not exist in earthly conditions. Let me explain. Sometimes, especially in youth, it is possible to dream of monsters whose physical form does not exist on earth. Those in lower levels of consciousness do this also. Similarly, in higher levels of mind there are souls whose beauty is beyond anything ever observed on earth.

If, then, mind can attract such conditions as to be surrounded by trees, flowers, birds, animals, etc., from where do these forms of life come? What force animates these forms of life? Equally, you may ask how it is possible for us to have soil, sand, rocks, mountains, rivers, seas and other inanimate forms. There is law and order even within the sub-atomic particles of one atom, the same as that found in a stone - mineral kingdom. This form of law and order could be said to be mind in its infancy. As we move from this kingdom to that of the plant and vegetable world, it can be seen that this mind has expanded to include the propagation of species as seen in the amoeba. It cannot die, but can indefinitely divide itself into two, thus ensuring preservation of its kind. As mind gradually evolves, the need for locomotion adds to the vehicle of matter. As we study the origin of species, we see how mind expands, realising that in order to develop higher senses, the need for male and female is being manifest. With this duality comes the chance for mind to expand even more, so that those levels of reasoning, intelligence, emotion and others appear in the animal kingdom. We, being a part of that kingdom, have developed mind to such a degree that it is capable of containing itself as an individual, so that in its eternal progress it may now develop that even finer level called love. It could be said that the etheric viscosity has become strong enough to preserve individuality.

When physical death occurs in any of these kingdoms, the controlling mind returns to that sea of mind appropriate to its development; like a drop of water falling back into the ocean. Thus there are seas of mind that belong to every physical manifestation on earth. By the creative ability of our individual minds, we may attract mind from any of these levels to animate etheric forms in our levels of consciousness. However, apart from this, those creatures to whom we gave love during earthly life can retain their individuality until we learn to put selfishness to one side, thus enabling them to return, adding their experience in that sea of mind to which they belong. Can all humans claim that their minds have reached a sufficient level of development as to retain individuality, or do some of lower mind lose it, their mind returning to the appropriate etheric sea? We are not able to give a finite answer to this question and feel those great souls who have understood some of these mysteries of creation have risen to levels beyond communication with your or my level. In all this eternal development of mind, the finger of God has indicated the pathway that the gradual manifestation of life has taken.

As I suggested, conditions in all our levels depend upon the desires and fantasies of those who dwell in each level. You may think that there could be nothing lower than some of those you see in your living world, those who commit crimes, murder, torture and other atrocious actions. Free of the physical body and earthly laws, those same minds can and do create conditions worse than anything observed on earth.

Where, then, is the butterfly world, the invisible world with its infinite levels of mind development? Answer - it is everywhere. Ether is everywhere in space - in matter, in the solar system and in infinity. The physical world is just one infinitesimal section in which the vibration of ether can be detected by physical senses. Even within one atom of matter there are particles that are invisible. The real you consists of these particles in a certain state of vibration. They do not find matter any obstacle whatsoever and, therefore, those particles lying closest to earth's vibrations may sometimes be perceived by a person whose sensitivity is high. That person may claim to have seen "a spirit" that was able to walk through a wall. If you could temporarily leave your physical body, you too could walk through the same wall. It is only the ball and chain of the physical body that prevents you.

All the levels of the butterfly world are therefore different states of vibration within the ether. Radio waves, gravitation, cohesion, magnetism and electricity are also vibrations of a different nature within the same ether. Different states of vibration within the physical world produce solids, liquids and gases. Likewise, different states of vibration within the ether produce different etheric states.

Just as in chemistry or physics you can change an invisible gas into liquid or solid by altering pressure and temperature, so we may alter the state of our vibration so as to become perceptible to certain sensitive minds. By dressing this etheric vibration within the physical substance exuded from certain physical persons, it is possible for us also to solidify in that process called materialisation.

Allow me, for a moment, to digress slightly in order to differentiate between what you call "spirit" and "ghost". That which you call "spirit" is, indeed, the etheric counterpart of an individual; that which you term "ghost" is an imprint upon the ether, just like a picture produced on light-sensitive paper - a photograph. It is but a shadow of the "spirit" left in a particular place, no doubt due to some shock or trauma at the time of transition from physical manifestation to etheric.

To return. In the first stages of leaving the earthly world and entering the invisible world, it is natural that mind still associates itself with this planet earth and therefore the location of the "spirit world" is earth - one of the seven parallel universes all in different states of vibration with, also, an infinite number of intermediate frequencies. Trying to explain this in earthly terms is difficult. Those in higher frequencies or spheres have put nearly all earthly memories to one side, yet retain all experiences gained in those lower levels. Do not, then, expect communication from such great souls, for they have shed many bodies including astral and etheric. No longer do they need form or shape. They are light, the luminosity of which is too intense for our eyes. What happens after one has passed through these seven spheres? Their connection with earth becomes more remote from one to seven. Creation is infinite. What lies outside the etheric gravitational attraction to earth we cannot say. We are told by intelligences greater than ourselves that progression and learning are infinite; we are all on an eternal journey. Is it not then sufficient to know that you survive after what is called "death", yet should be called "rebirth"? We will suggest some possible proof of this in the ensuing chapter. Some may wonder what would happen to these seven spheres if, for some cosmic reason, earth ceased to exist. If and when this occurs, there would be an immediate exodus from earthly to etheric existence and, therefore, that tie or attraction to earth would no longer be necessary; all that you love would be with you in etheric realms. All butterflies seem to find another garden should you destroy all the flowers in yours. The finger of God would, I am sure, once again point in the direction of that other garden in which they could continue their life.

What, then, do we do in this our invisible world? The answer to this question is obviously complex. When you receive communication from any of our levels, no doubt you feel some statements would contradict others. This is because the conditions that prevail in one level are different from those in another. The knowledge of those in higher spheres is such that they are able to give a greater truth than we can. Rather as religious and other concepts of those on earth differ, so the ideas of those in the etheric worlds may seem to be different. Let me therefore only transmit that which I know to be true, and not give just my own view.

The father of this channel did commit suicide - this topic merits a chapter of its own. After he received help and guidance from his "mentors", he was able to see that by such an action he did not escape from anything. The mental torment and physical suffering that he had before death simply changed in its proportion. I take a liberty here to explain fully how this change took place. During the final chapter of his physical life the father sustained a broken leg due to a motor cycle accident The bones failed to knit together properly and there was a possibility that some grafting would have to be done. At the same time, he became aware that his wife was not as faithful as he thought. Depression clouded his mind, causing him to take his own life by gassing himself. Having cast off his physical shell, he found that although his etheric double was perfect, the mental distress had increased. He had not changed the ways of his wife and now, with help and guidance, he realised that he had deserted a sinking ship. His family, including this channel, dearly missed him. He had shrunk away from the challenges that God's nursery school gave him. His recourse was to decide to try to help others on earth not to make the same mistake. If they did, he and his group would be there to meet them, to persuade them to help in the same way as he does. This he will continue to do until the time arrives for him to feel that he is ready to move onwards.

As for myself, I can count myself fortunate in the fact that I was able to stay the full course in that nursery school bringing with me that desire to blend science and religion. I therefore have set myself a double task of trying to influence men of science to see that infinity stretches two ways and also, using those few available channels through which we try to give truth, light and hope to you on earth - our spiritual family, for we are all part of that great incomprehensible whole.

Without digressing too much, let me expand a little on the duality of infinity. Here I may only express an opinion. Turn the telescope of your mind towards space and see that our earth in its solar system is an insignificant speck in that galaxy called the Milky Way. That galaxy with all its suns, solar systems and other cosmic manifestations is but one galaxy within the perception of the instruments of modern astronomers. To those astronomers I would now ask the question "Why only one big bang?" Maybe big bangs have always been and will always be. Now turn that telescope inwards to see that a single atom is a universe in itself. It is my opinion that if scientists continue to disassemble sub-atomic particles, they will not only discover more, but each time of a finer nature and vibration. They would be approaching the ether - our world. Those who are fortunate enough to separate the finer vibrations of mind from the lower, find themselves able to look at the results of those lower vibrations - their physical bodies. The finer vibrations constitute the invisible world. The lower vibrations of the other control that which is called matter.

Now to return, once again, to what we do in this - the real world. Everyone who enters our worlds eventually pass through a similar journey to that of the father and myself. All of my family and friends have likewise decided the best way, the best activity that would ensure their eternal progression. I will not invade the privacy of those relations and friends in enumerating their actions since arriving in etheric dimensions. Let it be sufficient to say that those in lower levels of mind do not "want to listen" - "and yet" eventually a light is seen, the light of those who have been trying to help them, both in the unreal and real world.

The universe consists of matter, motion, mind and spirit. In physical science we concern ourselves with matter and motion, ignoring those qualities associated with mind and spirit. In trying to explain conditions of mind and spirit, we realise that physical man naturally thinks in terms of matter and motion. If the butterfly tried to communicate with the caterpillar, describing the new world in which it finds itself, no doubt the caterpillar would want to relate and compare it with the cabbage leaf. A similar task lies before us. How do we describe the gardens of the invisible world when we have only experienced the flowers in one or two gardens?

In dreams, one seems to be able to communicate with others without having to speak as you do on earth. Who can claim to be

41

aware of time or night in dreams? Similarly, one can move from one part of the world to another without having to use any form of transport. As I make these statements, I feel some minds transmitting the fact that they have dreamt of forms of transport. That is true, yet on earth transport is necessary. Here it is not. If, in your level, it is your desire to create, as in dreams, some form of locomotion, then it is so. Those conditions of night, transport, sleep, food, drink and others that exist on earth are not necessities here. Depending upon the level of mind, one learns that those things that were necessary in earthly life are not needed here. I have already mentioned that my son communicated the fact that he could have a whisky and soda in his level at the time. Now he is spiritually teetotal. Do not feel that I am saying that the invisible world is a dream world. I am saying that the conditions here are more similar to the dream world in many respects than they are to earthly conditions. In dreams, is it not true that you sometimes feel emotion and love for those in your dream; that your companion or wife may sometimes not be part of your dream? You may dream on five consecutive nights without including your wife or husband as part of those dreams. Remember five earthly nights correspond to five or even fifty years in our world.

Is it surprising, then, that those who have gone before you, even though you shared great love for one another, never seem successfully to turn their spiritual eyes in your direction? They are still flying in their new garden, but will one day remember the cabbage leaf that they once left. It is possible that, before the remembrance takes place, you too will have become another butterfly in their world, able to fly with them, tasting the pollen of the beautiful flowers in one of God's infinite gardens. I must add one more fact. At physical birth there are parents, relations and friends there to welcome the new-born child. So in the butterfly world there are other butterflies to welcome you as you emerge from the cocoon of your physical shell.

To give some sense of reality to the level in which I now find myself, perhaps it would help if I gave an idea of all the activities I pursue in what on earth would be termed a daily routine. I have already stated that, in our levels, the existence of everything is due to the creative mind ability of the inhabitants. There is therefore a duplicate of all that existed on earth, constantly modified by those who join our sphere of consciousness. I can, and still do, enjoy a game of golf in conditions that are similar to those that prevail in Hoylake, Clouds, Gullane, Sutton Coldfield and other places where my friends take me. At Mariemont, I used to play tennis, for that gave greater exercise than golf. So it is that I still pursue recreational activities including, of course, music. It was my desire to become an accomplished pianist but, due to my multitude of interests, I only ever reached an elementary standard. Since those days, I have learnt much and now enjoy periods of improving my playing to include some of the works of Mozart, Chopin, Liszt and other great composers. My work in science still finds an outlet in the facility of adding my thoughts to your men of science. It may be interesting to some that I and other friends helped in the protection from heat of space craft. I still have a laboratory and can experiment in a similar manner to your earthly physicists and, if the outcome of my work is successful, then I try to impinge my thoughts on the minds of those engaged in similar work. The pressure of earthly activities did not permit me to spend much time in my gardens; only in retirement at Normanton House did I have the opportunity to bathe in the glory of the plant and vegetable world. Here, where earthly time has faded, the new freedom permits me to move from one interest to another without the handicaps of family responsibilities, financial concern, bodily health or political and religious concerns. We have unrestricted abilities to overcome all inhibitions. There is a desire level in each level of consciousness and in it we may fulfill those desires that earthly time prevented.

Naturally, the desires of those in high level of mind are of a more spiritual nature than those in levels closer to earth vibrations. Many of you are aware that the latter half of my earthly existence was spent pursuing a conviction of the survival of human personality. Now that I am here, I try to pass my verification of this fact through those channels who are willing to listen and yet, although many feel the call, few are chosen as suitable. I can meet all the friends that I ever knew and endeavour to put right the misunderstandings that I had with those with whom I disagreed.

Apart from all these activities, I share the knowledge of those in different groups. I am privileged to listen to those whose minds reside in much higher levels than ours; those who teach us to communicate by colour, music, pictorial visual transmission of thought and the emotion within our minds. I give lectures to those who now desire to understand the scientific principles within physics and chemistry. Yes, although some individuals have left earth dimensions, they realise that some of the lessons learnt in earthly conditions must be understood before laws of invisible dimensions can be understood. One must learn simple arithmetic before an attempt can be made to appreciate abstract mathematics.

There are many subjects that I did not have an opportunity of studying. I now take the opportunity of listening to others speaking on biology, medicine, cosmology and a host of most interesting topics. I feel that it is necessary to understand totally life, with all its relative knowledge before one can understand death with all its implications. The butterfly must first exist as a caterpillar.

My life then involves teaching, learning, playing, sharing, meeting old friends, meeting new friends and travelling upwards along that infinite spiritual pathway. Each step we take makes it more difficult to communicate with those human caterpillars still crawling in earthly dimensions. What lies ahead in the continuum of creation I do not know. Does the infant know what it is like to be a wise old man? I am still an infant butterfly, learning to use my wings as I fly from one opportunity to another. Speaking metaphorically, I am told that one day I will not even need wings to fly, but I cannot imagine the conditions that will prevail when that day arrives.

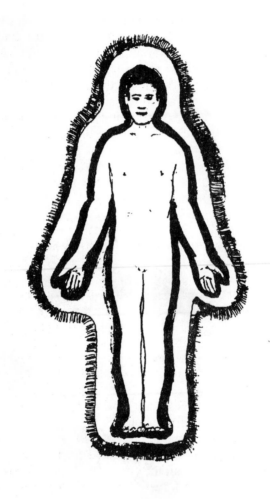

Body, Etheric, Mind and Spirit

Chapter 3

BODY, ETHERIC, MIND AND SPIRIT

Many people engaged in the research of mediumship often refer to body, etheric, mind and spirit, yet I feel that the definition of each needs some clarification. Before I use these terms again within the chapters that follow, allow me to try to give some meaning to them. In many of my books I postulated the theory that the substance ether is the link between that which is visible to the physical and that which is invisible. My ideas concerning this have not changed - merely expanded. Allow me, then, to share thoughts with you of the relationship between these four vibrations.

Just as invisible steam condenses into water by cooling, in the same way ether substance condenses into what is called matter. This is achieved by a reduction of vibrations. If the vibratory state of ether is increased, then we have an even finer substance which the qualities of mind use. The most pure substance of all is that which lies even above the mind substance and is known as spirit. Spirit and mind are certainly invisible but, when clothed with an etheric covering, can be seen by those earthly beings called sensitives.

Each of these for very different states afford their own particular qualities. In the case of matter, it is known that it manifests as a large number of chemical elements which, by different combinations, form everything of which man is aware in this and other solar systems. This, of course, includes his own physical body as well as all other animate and inanimate manifestations. Spirit, mind and etheric all exist in both the animate and inanimate, but naturally in varying proportions. It is necessary to take each of the four and try to discover their function within creation.

Even within the realms of matter, there are varying states of vibrations shown by the different numbers of electrons in their atomic structure; these constitute all the chemical elements known to science and again display themselves either solid, liquid or gas. Thus, within matter exists all that may be perceived in both nature and science, whether organic or inorganic, whether living or seemingly devoid of life.

There does seem to be some law or order even within a single atom and, therefore, it could be said that mind in an elementary form exists within the mineral kingdom. This low order of mind simply maintains stability instead of chaos. Without it the particles of an atom could not exist together. If any form of mind does exist within the mineral kingdom, then it requires ether as a link between mind and matter. A stone is therefore essentially matter, ether and very elementary mind, whereas earthly man consists of matter, ether, highly evolved mind and even that higher vibrational substance termed spirit. The kingdoms of plant, vegetable and animal lie in between those of the mineral and human, with their appropriate ingredients of mind and spirit. The matter or physical world, linked through the etheric, gives mind an opportunity to expand until it is strong enough to retain its individuality. Then its vibrations are high enough to include that higher level called spirit.

We have said that the matter world is divided into various elements. Similarly, the etheric substance provides an opportunity for sub-division. Electricity, magnetism, gravity, light and cohesion all use etheric substance as a medium for their various energies and forces. Man has learnt how to use electricity to produce magnetism, light and heat but has yet to master the full forces of gravity and cohesion. The processes of materialisation and de-materialisation are simply the changing from etheric frequencies to the matter world and vice versa. The matter world cannot exist without the forces within the ether, but the etheric world does exist without having to make use of matter. Likewise, mind substance exists independently of the etheric world but makes use of ether in order to affect matter. The world of spirit, in a similar way, uses mind and ether to manifest in the world of matter: - I am. It is well known that some sensitives can hold some earthly object and feel vibrations coming from that object in a science called psychometry. With regard to this, I would stress that such feelings come from the etheric vibrations of that object rather than its physical part.

Thoughts from the mind world often make an imprint on ether no matter whether that ether is located in a room or a personal possession; hence ghosts and psychometry. The etheric world is then both within and without everything that is visible or invisible. Those of us who still clothe our mind substance with ether can still retain memories to do with the earthly existence that we have left, but those existing in the higher dimensions of mind have put aside their etheric garment, retaining only the wisdom and experience gained in both physical and etheric worlds.

Even the mind world is divided into many levels of consciousness - those who have just shed their etheric layer and those who have raised themselves high enough to appreciate fully the world of spirit; a world of pure and divine love. Of this world I have no knowledge, only that by being of continual service I will one day attain the privilege of becoming pure spirit - pure light.

Life force, or the animate, therefore consists of matter, ether and mind that needs locomotion for its learning. The inanimate part of the physical world contains matter, ether and mind in such a low level that locomotion would serve no purpose. Mind, then, with the guidance of spirit, gradually moves from inanimate to animate to etheric and so on, in its eternal journey. On this journey, mind, as it progresses, puts aside the necessity of the physical world and even the use of the etheric, as it moved towards the vibrations of pure spirit.

In transmitting these thoughts to you, I must again bring to your mind the fact that what you read comes from not only myself, but a group, as well as the higher thoughts of one who we call "The Great Light". Today's scientists are at last discovering that particles of different vibrations and behaviour exist even within that single atom. One day they may agree that those particles or waves could be the essences of matter, ether, mind and spirit. With the dawn of that day will come the blending of scientific and religious thought. The laws of quantum mechanics cannot explain all waves within creation. There are laws that exist beyond these laws - the laws that govern emotion, appreciation of beauty and love. These qualities are of the mind and spirit, they cannot be measured or researched by any scientific instruments.

From the preceding paragraphs, I hope that it may be seen that the mind of mankind has journeyed through those lower kingdoms of mineral, vegetable and animal. Man's mind has grown beyond the simple law and order within the atom, beyond those slightly higher laws of self-preservation and now vibrates in higher frequencies that include reasoning, intellect, emotion and love. The planet earth is a wonderful panorama showing mind in its infinite forms of development, yet I sometimes feel that man cannot see its full beauty. This beauty is obscured by the physical clouds of earthly technology. It is time mankind realised that all that he has was provided by that great infinite mind that, for want of a better word, we all call God. As for the true appreciation of that infinite mind, we are just as mystified as when we lived in the earthly dimension.

With regard to the minds that exist in those lower kingdoms, especially those that fall in the category of animate, I assure you that all survive. Those who have received love will, for a time, retain their individuality before joining that level of consciousness to which they belong. They are like the raindrops that eventually fall back into the sea. The invisible world consists of an infinite number of these seas of consciousness.

To summarise: In earthly dimensions, the inanimate embraces matter, ether, mind (in the form of law and order) and unawakened spirit. The animate part of the earth contains matter which, through ether, is controlled by mind that has developed sufficiently to need locomotion. These forms of life manifest with minds in infinite levels of development, the highest being mankind, in whom spiritual vibrations have begun to shine. Outside earthly dimensions are etheric levels, once again with many or infinite levels of consciousness. Those who inhabit the highest etheric realms do not need to carry specific earthly memories - only the experience gained. This experience enables them to shed their etheric covering so that they may journey through those mental spheres towards those of pure light - the spiritual or celestial spheres from which pure and divine love radiates.

Having expressed some thoughts on the consistency of matter, etheric, mind and spirit, we are more able to answer some of those questions that we received from the mind of this instrument. In the following chapter, we will present those questions, then proceed to give a meaningful answer, hoping that his questions may be the same as yours.

Questions and Answers

Chapter 4

QUESTIONS AND ANSWERS

QUESTION 1

Why is it that we have such things as Siamese twins and babies born with what are termed physical or mental deformities?

ANSWER

You may equally ask whether all clovers have four leaves and whether these abnormalities of nature exist within other kingdoms. The answer to this question is not singular but complex, for there are many reasons why the vehicle of life is not always in a form that is considered to be the norm. In the first place, consider the fact that if everything in the earthly world was in the same state, there would be no means of comparison. Only by observing that others around you are better or worse equipped physically and mentally are you able to exercise those levels of mind called reasoning - emotional and inspirational. Is the genius considered to be abnormal? There are individuals in earthly life who have not manifested in human form before as, in the same way, there are some who have brought with them the experiences gained in many incarnations. That infinite intelligence we call God, in his wisdom, saw that in the earthly nursery school these situations were necessary for man's learning and progression. The differences in mental ability are there to encourage you to help those less fortunate than yourself and/or to give you the aspiration to become as good as those who are more advanced. Not only in the invisible world are there "many mansions" but also in the visible world. The level of a person's mind must not be judged by their ability to express themselves, for that ability may be impaired by their physical body - principally the brain organ.

As for differences in the body, how could you ever fully appreciate the facility of the five senses if there were no blind, deaf, dumb or others afflicted in other ways? The main bodily organ through which the mind expresses itself is, of course, the brain. This organ may, even at birth, be deficient of cells that contribute towards the use of these five senses. Just as that clover may have three or five leaves, other organs of the body can develop in abnormal condition. This may be due to "the sins of the fathers"; in other words, the parents and ancestors could have abused their bodily vehicles so as to interfere with the patterns that govern normality of the body; another lesson in this nursery school - respect the vehicle of the mind and spirit.

There are, however, even other reasons why such abnormalities occur in life. In certain cases, I understand that it is possible for a soul to undergo the frustration of not having sufficient means whereby it may express itself. This is because, in previous experiences, that soul was always unsympathetic to people with afflictions. Only by having such a personal experience will this spirit be able, eventually, to leave behind these necessary earthly trials. In all cases of manifestation of life, mind and spirit are attracted to the vehicle and in every case the mind needs the experiences afforded by that vehicle. This applies not only to the human species but to all forms of life. There are natural laws in the invisible world governing these processes, just as earthly laws govern all that is called matter.

Before proceeding with other questions, I would remind you once again that these thoughts are those of our group, not only the thoughts of one with the label "Lodge".

QUESTION 2

Is this planet earth the only one with life on it?

ANSWER

Once again, a complex question that necessitates a complex answer. This planet earth is but one in our solar system. Our solar system is one of trillions in that one galaxy called the Milky Way. Similarly, that galaxy is but one of trillions within the range of the instruments of modern astronomers. The reason why life manifested on this particular planet is because the conditions relating to its mass and distance from the sun are conducive to the formation of an atmosphere that is necessary to support life as you know it. Logically, life in different forms with different conditions have similarly formed in other parts of creation; some of that life is governed by minds far more advanced than any within these seven earthly spheres, and other planets no doubt lag behind the development witnessed on earth. Man in his innate vanity seems to delude himself that God created the universe so that this one planet earth could support life. Those of us who are privileged to communicate with you are naturally still within the boundaries of those spheres linked to earth and, therefore, may only pass to you thoughts from those in higher states of consciousness. The fish of the sea live in different conditions than those of mankind, yet they live. Life in other parts of creation, with different conditions, surely manifests. It would seem that God, the farmer, prepared the field before sowing the seeds of life in it. Often one field lies dormant whilst seeds are set in another. Galaxies collapse whilst others are born.

With regard to the varieties of skin, culture and modes of life, would life not be duller if there were only one type of rose, fish, bird, insect or animal? Again, that infinite intelligence knew that mind needed such a variety of conditions for its manifestation, progress and learning.

QUESTION 3
How can I really prove life after death?

ANSWER
You can't. My friend Myers devoted his life to the proof of survival and even after his death hoped that the cross-correspondences would demonstrate his continuation in the invisible world. Communications I received from Myers, my aunt Anne, my son Raymond and many others, gave sufficient evidence for me to conclude that their minds still existed in another dimension. I stress "I was able to conclude", for I feel that, even to-day, proof is a more private affair than public. In many books that I wrote I gave the opinion that no single experience could ever give this finite proof. Only the gathering of evidence from many different sources and various phenomena would help to give you the proof you seek. If there were a multitude of brilliant mediums on earth then there would be no need to seek and find - there would be no need for hope. Looking back, I can see that part of the divine plan is to make mankind puzzled by all the mysteries surrounding both birth and death. If man knew for certain all the conditions that prevail in our worlds, he may decide to put an end to the challenges of earthly life. Accept, then, that mankind was meant to have one eye on earthly conditions and the other on those happenings that cannot be explained by physics or any other earthly science.

If you have read well, you will be aware that during my life there were some very good - no, excellent - mediums, both mental and physical, yet their work only gave proof, through evidence, to a few of us. I personally feel that in aeons of time, if and when evidence, therefore proof, is in great abundance, then this particular solar system will have served its purpose. In the meantime, man must continue to ask and receive, seek and find, all the secrets and mysteries of both life and death. Those who are fully aware of cause and effect will already have concluded that physical existence must have a purpose, and that this purpose is a preparation for that which is to follow.

Many in the invisible world constantly strive to find different ways of making mankind aware of their presence. If one way seems to fail, then another way is found. You now have more varieties of phenomena than we ever had. As the number of good mental and physical mediums seem to diminish, other phenomena gradually take their place - I refer to the examples of clinical death, death-bed visions, electronic audio and visual phenomena, strange patterns in cornfields, some strange objects in the sky that seem to have surpassed the speed of light, and a host of other phenomena. Sufficient for us to say that, as man advances technologically, we try to take advantage of using this advancement to show that not all phenomena can be explained by the science of earth.

QUESTION 4

Is there such a thing as fate? Are our lives planned and, if so, by whom?

ANSWER

When having the privilege of transmitting thoughts to groups of people, I often say "There is no such thing as coincidence". One cannot answer a simple "Yea" or "Nay" to this question, for much explanation is required. First, with regard to coincidence and fate, I bring to your notice another poem that my son Raymond has put together:-

Lincoln and Kennedy with names of seven
Both now reside in the very same heaven.
They were both loving, peaceful and kind -
Bullets into both heads their way did find.
Their two wives were witness of their killing,
Coincidence of this tale is chilling.
They came into office a century apart,
On a Friday both new lives did start.
Number of names their assassins had three,
Oswald shot Kennedy - Booth, Lincoln's soul set free.
One fired his gun in a theatre and fled
To a store that may be called a shed.

From a store the other did fire,
Then to a theatre did retire.
Neither of them came to trial,
Their birth dates a century different on file.
Both Presidents their office did start
Exactly one hundred years apart.
Lincoln's secretary one called Kennedy was resident,
Kennedy's secretary same name as other President.
Lincoln was in Ford theatre when shot,
Kennedy into Ford Lincoln car he got.
Their successors born century apart they claim,
What do you think? - They had the same name.
They were called Johnson and both came from the South
Does this coincidence leave open your mouth?
The two Presidents each knew of their fate
Told by those this side of the gate.
If in your life there be patterns the same
There is much more to life than just a name.

To answer your question. If you can accept that the planet earth is one of God's nursery schools, then you must equally accept that this school provides opportunities for the mind to progress through the experiences that physical manifestation provides. There are certain lessons that the soul may learn only by utilising the vehicle called body, and by the advice of those wiser than ourselves we become aware of the lessons not yet learnt. When we are born we bring with us an inner knowledge of those experiences that are necessary for the progression of the mind. There is therefore a plan - a path chosen by ourselves - that will provide those necessary lessons. It may be that the mind lacks the quality of patience, in which case the pathway chosen will be full of experiences that would exercise the use of this quality. Those on this particular journey would not have an easy life. Imagine, then, that in each life there are certain stepping stones upon which the individual must tread in order to cross life's river. How one goes from one stone to another enables the individual to exercise free will. One may take an easy or hard route from one stone to another; one may fall off a stone many times and either give up or try again, knowing that, eventually, the river must be crossed. If the river is not crossed this time, then the same untrodden stones will be there in the next earthly journey. On these crossings, some would seem to have large, easily surmounted stones,

57

whilst others have tiny stones that make the journey very arduous. Those on the easy pathway may help those on a harder crossing, as some may have done this crossing many times before and can benefit others by their experience. It is felt by our group that there is a plan for each life, but how that plan is put into effect depends upon the free will of each individual.

Before incarnation, a soul knows what lessons are needed and therefore plans which crossing would afford the best opportunity for learning. This plan is very complex, for it even involves the planetary influences at the time of birth. No one can doubt that those born at the same time and in the same place would have certain similar qualities. This astrological influence is also part of the same plan. It could be that man has to master all the qualities associated with all of the birth signs. In a similar fashion, one is born with a certain surname with its vibrations which can influence the bodily vehicle. All these things, and many more, are taken into consideration in determining the size of the stones upon which man must tread in life's crossing. From these observations, it could be concluded that the harder journey is of more benefit to the soul and that, in life, one should not envy those who seem to be "born with a silver spoon in their mouth". It is then ourselves, with advice, who govern our own destiny.

QUESTION 5

What age are you now? Tell me about age in your world.

ANSWER

As you know by your reading, I moved from your dimension to this one when my physical body had served me for eighty-nine years. As you are aware, other souls make the same journey after a very short earthly life. In conversations on earth regarding age, it is the age of the bodily vehicle that is considered, whereas here, in our dimensions, other factors are taken into consideration.

Remember that here the mind is clothed with an etheric garment and therefore we must make comment on both mind and its etheric covering. As for the mind, it is as old as its development through all kingdoms, as well as its many human incarnations. A more apt description of mind would be in words that referred to its experience and wisdom. I am sure that you are familiar with that expression used to describe a very young child - "He or she is an old soul", meaning, of course, that the child seems to bring with it experience and even knowledge that it could not possibly have assimilated in the short period after birth. One only has to think of Mozart. The age of my mind, therefore, goes back to a time when its development deserved individualisation.

When I first came into invisible dimensions, naturally my etheric double was a duplicate of the earthly body I had left behind. As one becomes quickly accustomed to this new butterfly world, one learns to manipulate that etheric covering to show an age that is appropriate for the situation. Take this instrument for example. When he makes his journey to our world, he will arrive in a level of consciousness where it is possible for his many relations and friends to greet him. He will not stay in this level, even though it is a level upon which all his friends can feel comfortable. Remember that those who meet him come from their own level, which may be higher or lower than that of Raymond's. They will, of course, present themselves in a form that Raymond will immediately recognise, for it would be no use his parents appearing at that meeting as if they were both in their teens. The etheric body, then, can be changed just as you change your earthly clothes. When there is no need to meet those travelling from earthly conditions, the etheric assumes a form that would be considered prime by the mind that governs that etheric semi-matter. Apart from this, there are other factors to be taken into consideration. The physical or mental handicaps of the earthly body no longer exist and those features that you did not like can, to some extent, be changed. To explain this properly, let us consider someone who on earth had a discolouration of skin, a broken nose or a face disfigured by an accident. This sight no longer prevails once the physical body is left behind. In fact, apart from this, as the mind and spirit grow wiser and become more spiritual, this is reflected in the etheric garment, until that garment is no longer needed. If I may be permitted to use my rather dry sense of humour, I am to-day more handsome than ever!

QUESTION 6

Should the medical profession and those knowledgeable of the human body, transplant human organs or use the eggs of one woman in another so that she may give birth?

ANSWER

We cannot answer for God. The answers that are given are only in the light of our own level of consciousness, combined with the wisdom of those whose light shines brighter. Should an appendix be removed? - often its removal prolongs the life of one who suffers appendicitis. The group here feels that all steps should be taken to ensure that the body remains a good instrument through which the soul may receive experiences as well as express itself. Those who study and repair the human body can only conclude that its design and function was brought about by an infinite intelligence. The body serves the purpose of locomotion. When a motor car ceases to be of use, the driver would be wise to get out and walk. Alternatively, if the vehicle can be repaired by replacements, then it enables the driver to continue his journey without having either to walk or buy a new car. Sometimes a driver may borrow another vehicle or even be given a ride in someone else's car, but this parallel becomes rather complex when applied to the soul or mind.

Now I would like to leave the questions that prevail in your minds, for as you will observe, for every problem that both you and we are able to solve satisfactorily, more questions seem to present themselves. Learning and understanding is truly an infinite task. It must be so since our journey has no end. Allow me, then, in the following chapters, to share more thoughts with you so that, in later chapters, we may discuss points that arise. We will once again present them in similar manner.

Memories and Reincarnation

Chapter 5

MEMORIES AND REINCARNATION

In physical life one passes through a maze of experiences as the chapters of life are lived. Some of you may be able to turn back those pages recalling incidents of the past whereas others would find this process more difficult. Which, I ask, is the more important - the memory or the experience gained by the individual? In that phenomenon called regression, I wonder whether any have been able to reach back to grasp memories of a life lived in the stone age era. Surely, if life is eternal our eyes should be more on what lies ahead, rather than trying to see that distant water that passed under the bridge long ago.

From the knowledge that I have gained with respect to these matters, I see clearly now that we only need carry with us those lessons that we did not manage to learn in the past. You are today - I am today - the result of all that we have learned in our eternal journey. For some of us, a vivid recall of a past life whilst in earthly dimension would interfere too much with the life we are living, whether in visible or invisible worlds. We drink the cup of forgetfulness with each rebirth, yet retain the spiritual nourishment of every experience. I realise that what I have just stated is supportive of reincarnation, so let me add the thoughts of the group assembled here to substantiate this view, for there are many implications.

First, with regard to memory, the instrument of the mind is, of course, the physical brain, rather similar to one of your modern computers. The five physical senses constitute the main keys of that computer, for it receives its information by means of stimulation by these senses. The physical brain behaves like a transmitter, transmitting the results of life's experiences to life's force field, the mind with its many layers. The mind may store exact information or just what has been learnt by an individual experience. When physical death takes place, the computer is detached from whatever machine has been used to record and store this information. In earthly life, you can take this information and use it with other computers, in the same way as we now use this channel. I understand that often such programmes are condensed or shortened so as to cast out that which is unnecessary - all the "buts", "ands", "fors", etc. In the gradual progression of mind, a similar process takes place so that only the essentials are kept and the garbage of individual happenings are discarded.

Some minds may want to keep memories of earthly incidents and lives for a long time, others may realise that, by keeping exact memories of all that happened in earthly dimension, their progress would be handicapped. Do not expect us all to be able to furnish you with exact memories of the life we have just left, for some of us have already put to one side those that we feel are a burden to carry. In the same way, although I know that our minds have evolved by journeying through all kingdoms - mineral, vegetable, animal and human - I feel that in the level on which we now exist, only the experiences of that last journey are kept. Can your mind reach back to the time when it was part of the plant and vegetable sea of mind? Mine can't.

In the evolution of our minds, I understand that even memories of language are discarded and that, in some lofty spheres of consciousness, communication takes place by telepathy, music, colour and even higher vibrations of emotion and feeling. If we could carry with us all memory of the past and reach out for an understanding of what lies ahead, then each of us would understand the history of evolution from alpha to omega. I wish that I could give you exact details of the stone age, on the construction of the pyramids and, equally, life in other galaxies, but I cannot. What has gone before simply laid the foundation for that which lies ahead. Like you, I know that I am and where I am - that is all. At the very start of this book were written the words "Do not expect us all mysteries to solve". I hope that from this you may understand why those on this side of the veil can only give to you glimpses of the life they left behind - not often their full names, addresses, telephone numbers and suchlike.

Now, that much-discussed "reincarnation". Because of concern for oneself, much of mankind tends only to associate this subject with whether or not they have lived other human lives. Surely this topic should also include all other kingdoms, including mineral. If life is eternal, should a dog always be a dog? Should an ant always be an ant? Logically, life on planet earth seems to have gradually evolved from something like a virus to what it is today. In this evolution, it would seem that, as mind gradually expanded, it needed an appropriate vehicle through which it could manifest and express itself, hence the theory of the evolution of species - "and yet" - there does seem to be a missing link between one species and another. The supply of the elements of mind is infinite, therefore there will always be the necessity of an infinite variety of vehicles. On earth, human form is recognised as the highest vehicle in which mind can express itself, yet not all living on earth are perfect. Not all living in etheric dimensions are perfect. Common sense would suggest that one earthly incarnation may not be sufficient for mind to benefit from all the lessons offered in that life. Can any of us truly say that we have mastered all the challenges that physical life has to offer? We are told that, for many, there comes an awareness that, before further progress may be made, there is a necessity to learn those lessons that can only be learnt in the physical world. Only when this has been achieved can we stay in mental spheres to continue our journey. This of course applies to all levels of consciousness, even in those lower kingdoms. When a certain molecule of mind in any kingdom develops sufficiently, it gravitates naturally to the next level, ready to be attracted to another suitable physical vehicle. I stress that, in those lower forms of life, it is a more natural process because mind has not really become totally aware of itself as an individual. The minds of mankind are different in the fact that they have now raised reason, intellect, emotion and finer vibrations to a sufficient level to deserve free will and individuality. This being so, there is a longer interim period between one physical incarnation and another than there is in the plant, insect, fish, bird and animal worlds.

In our world, we realise that we are part of a great spiritual family; a family more close than earthly families. Some of this family are in etheric wavelengths whilst others have returned to gather more experience from the lessons presented in physical incarnation. You may call us guides, helpers, inspirers and other names, but we are simply part of a great family, anxious to try to help those members of the same family who have returned once more to earth to learn. We in the invisible world benefit from those experiences our earthly family undergo. One day, the level of mind in which I and my friends exist will reach a stage when none of us will need to dress ourselves with earthly flesh. There will be even greater tasks and challenges in those spheres of light that lie ahead of us.

And so, a dog is not always a dog; an ant is not always an ant. Our minds have travelled a long journey from the time when we were part of only law and order - that observed in a single atom - to now, when that law and order has added to itself the ability to manifest in matter. Having done so, that initial vibration had added to itself more and more layers until that time when it could be called mind. In order to learn and expand, mind needed locomotion; it needed to be able to preserve its own species. Eventually, in its expansion came male and female, giving mind greater opportunities - maybe this was the beginning of love in animalistic fashion. Which one of us when living on earth would truly lay down his life for another? Only your earthly family. The understanding of love must raise itself higher than this before we are free of all earthly feelings and lessons.

Not all your invisible friends are in higher levels of mind than yourself. Birds of a feather...... Some are on the same level as yourself, able to influence you telepathically. Others on higher levels work with them in an effort to try to be of service - one of the greatest qualities in the enhancement of love. We are all part of an infinite system of vibrations. Like dust in a cinema, we are seen for a while, then pass out of sight for a while to join the great whole. We may have to pass in and out of that light many times, until we escape from the confines of that earthly building. A day will come when vibrations affect our dusty particle and we are dust no more, but something much finer.

A light much brighter than my own would say to us, "Which name would you like to call me - that which earthly friends would call me in one life, or do you prefer the name I was given in another? Do you prefer me to dress in etheric robes of male or female?" That particular soul is no longer a butterfly, for that light no longer needs an etheric garment. As purity of spirit is slowly gained, such garments are no longer needed, for pure spirit has no form, no sex, no name - just light.

Do you really want to stay the same for ever? You might, but another soul undergoing the lessons of poverty, blindness, mental or physical handicaps, may not. Try to be understanding of those around you who are possibly struggling to express themselves. If you succeed, then you obviate having to struggle in similar manner. In the same way, see that you have already passed - reincarnated through all those lower kingdoms of life that you see around you.

However, let me reassure you that the bonds of love that you have formed for those who have already returned home will ensure that they will stay in invisible dimensions until you are able to leave the cabbage leaf of life and join them. As I understand it, reincarnation only takes place when the time is right; when you have spent sufficient time to realise its necessity. In countries that accept the reality of this, the time between one appearance on earth and another is drastically reduced. There are also great lights who, from time to time, choose to incarnate, praying that by so doing they may help to rid earth of its scourges of materialism, selfishness, jealousy and war.

I still uphold the view that, in the beginning of this solar system everything was inanimate and owed its origin to a nebula. The fiery mass broken off the sun by tidal action is one small ingredient in the multifarious phenomena that exist today. There was also a multitude of spiritual influences that took the opportunity of incorporating with matter, knowing that this would afford that essence of spirit a chance to progress. This theory holds good, not only for this solar system, but for all matter that has formed from the energy of creation. It seems that infinite mind-God is on an eternal adventure and that we are one very small part of it. Reincarnation is therefore a means by which this spiritual essence may combine with different vehicles of matter, sometimes taking an opportunity to change and improve the vehicles that it uses. It is not limited to this section of creation but, once free of the seven auric spheres of earth, moves on - to what? It is my hypothesis that, in other sections of creation there are greater challenges than those we experience here.

Before moving on, I remind you that the intelligence and thought expressed in these chapters is not only my own (Oliver Lodge), but that of a group assembled here for the purpose of trying to enlighten those who are willing to listen. If I repeat the story of my life - Comb Rectory Birds Destruction Society - this channel will be accused of researching into books written about me. A far better purpose is served as I combine my thoughts with others. This time, I feel that the same and greater truth is expressed in a more simplistic style. Do not therefore expect to see such words as "Epiphenomenalism". Not many understood such words before. I have learned much since the ball and chain of my body was removed - now I fly free like the butterfly, in a world beyond the comprehension of the caterpillar.

I want to express the thoughts of all my friends in the group. We realise that, if we were to continue transmitting our feelings about reincarnation, nothing more would be achieved. Those who have the final answer to this perplexing question are in levels of mind beyond our understanding. For the moment then, allow those cases, especially in India, that are suggestive of reincarnation to be sufficient to at least allow its possibility. With these and the fact that many living people claim memories of other incarnations, it does seem to be a subject worthy of further study.

Finally, I am given to understand that, before reincarnating, there would be a rest period, a falling into unconsciousness, when memories of the time spent in the etheric world fade. Those on earth who have a severe accident often lose memory of trauma, thus enabling them to continue their life without the shock and stress sustained. Before rebirth, a similar process takes place. If we could, at birth, bring with us full memory of whence we came, then maybe we would not want to stay amidst the trials and tribulations of earthly life. Let us move on. It would seem, from what I am told, that earthly life may be compared with the actors of old who held a mask in front of their face to portray a certain character. In the next play they would use a different mask in order to hide their true personalities. Having obtained individuality, it seems that the many earthly lives are like the masks of the actor. When we have mastered all the challenges of life, we need act no more. We can put all the masks down and enter a new theatre in which masks are not necessary. The actor may now show his true face and personality.

Guides

Chapter 6

GUIDES

Without any wish to offend those who feel that they have a highly evolved soul guiding their life, I would like to make some comments on these matters. In previous chapters, we have tried to explain that natural laws pervade in invisible dimensions just as they do in physical life. There are, of course, differences for, in earthly life, one cannot always be with friends who think and behave in the same way as oneself. As I have already stated, here we live in a level of consciousness where thought and behaviour are nearly the same. The slight variations enable us to gather in groups in which all have the same interests, desires and choice of the way that we may be of service to others. Because of this, it is not necessary for each of us to have an individual teacher. One suffices for each group. Besides this, we share our knowledge and experience with other groups in our dimension so that every group benefits from one another.

Conditions on earth are so different. It could be said that there are as many religions or philosophies as there are people. This is one reason why those living on earth each need an individual guardian. Just as parents and teachers on earth try to influence children to make wise decisions in their life, so those who have chosen to act as your guardian try telepathically to influence your mind. This advice may be either heeded or ignored in both your dimension and ours. Free will is a means by which we are able to make mistakes; from those wrong decisions, we gradually learn to become wiser. Do you really feel that every thought that enters your mind originates from yourself? If one admits telepathy, then surely many thoughts come from those both incarnate and discarnate. Those who have chosen to act as your mentors are, naturally, souls who are on a similar mind frequency to yourself. If this were not so, no thoughts could be passed from their minds to yours. At the same time, it must be said that the teacher should not only be wiser than the student, but also be able to make the student understand the lessons given. If you claim that your guide is very highly evolved, then it is necessary for your mind to be developed to a level that is capable of understanding those higher philosophies.

In universities on earth there is usually one principal whose job it is to see that you are provided with the specialists that suit your course of study. As you progress mentally and spiritually, your guardian will bring in helpers from time to time to help you understand those various chapters of your earthly life. For this to occur, you must have a thirst for learning. Those who ask will receive, but must be prepared to suffer the pain of learning. To give this some real meaning, let us explain how we came as a group to work with this particular channel.

The guardian of this instrument knew that he would make the study of mind his lifetime work. Because of this, it was necessary for him to work amongst others - hence the choice of school teaching. The inclusion of music helped to develop character and self-discipline. Then came the mutual interest of how the mind could affect the body - the study of hypnosis. Time spent sailing helped to give him a respect of nature and, therefore, God. It was seen that sensitive vibrations might one day enable him to enter a trance-like state. That was when one who calls himself Phillippe agreed to help inject those more feminine, intuitive and emotional vibrations into his mind. Phillippe's earthly names were Armand Jacques Marie Chasenet, rather a mouthful. Those who choose to help do not always give their earthly names. There is a sensible reason for this. It was realised that this channel developed the desire to blend scientific reasoning with all that he had acquired in his study of religion. That was when I felt that here was an opportunity to share my thoughts with regard to this. I am therefore just one helper in the group in which we all play our part on the stage of Raymond's life.

In my opinion, very few people are aware of their actual guardian; they are more aware of those advisers that are brought in as specialists in their own field of knowledge. If you knew the name and last incarnation of your "mentor", you may take greater interest in their last earthly journey rather than in the guidance that they try to give. Some may even boast that they have a wise Indian or Chinese guide, feeling that by having such a counsellor, they must be wiser than those who have an Irish, German or even English guardian. The wise man is the man who realises that he is only a drop of water in the infinite ocean of creation. I therefore implore you to listen constantly to the thoughts that are given from invisible dimensions, instead of putting the emphasis on the personality of the transmitter.

We are all complex beings with many levels of mind. The lower levels are always subject to influences from our low levels of consciousness. Those who act as your guardians cannot always shield you from these influences; this is necessary so that you may exercise your free will either to submit to temptation or rise above it. Only as mind progresses does it learn to ignore thoughts that come from those in lower levels.

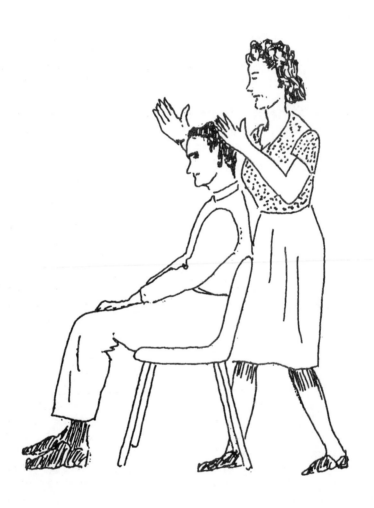

Prayer and Healing

Chapter 7

PRAYER AND HEALING

PRAYER

We are often asked to make comment as to whether prayer serves any useful purpose and, if so, to whom prayer should be directed. Allow us then to include our thoughts on this matter.

Throughout the past, tribal leaders have no doubt prayed to God for victory against their enemies, yet in any war, only one side may be victorious. The victors felt that God was on their side whilst the defeated felt that they had displeased God. For centuries mankind has prayed for peace, yet war, aggression, torture, greed and jealousy still seem as prevalent as ever. We are aware that in Spiritualism and other religions, prayers include the welfare of the animal kingdom as well as those parts of the world that suffer from drought, earthquakes, famine and other natural disasters. One would have thought that if God were a personified being, then all the wars, earthquakes and other plagues of society would have finished long ago; nay - never have started. If God were as benevolent and loving as is suggested in the scriptures, then mankind should have lived in a "Utopia" world ever since his first appearance on earth. Why should you have to pray that "God's will be done on earth as it is in heaven"? In fact, is it true that God's will prevails in heaven? From my observation it does not. Let us try to make some sense of all this by first defining what is meant by God.

I repeat that just as in physical birth, in rebirth (death), one finds oneself in a state of consciousness with other people who eventually help you to realise that you have left the handicaps of physical life. The butterfly has no greater conception of God than the caterpillar. It simply finds itself in a completely new environment where it is able to enjoy greater freedom. In a similar manner we, irrespective of which level of consciousness we find ourselves in, have no greater understanding of God and creation than we had when living on the cabbage leaf of earth. In fact, for some, the greater freedom is so overwhelming that they temporarily forget those they have left behind. Even in this new world, we feel that an understanding of God and creation lies far beyond our spiritual grasp. It is said that the workman is known by his work. If these infinite levels of mind are the work of God, then God is something far greater than I could ever appreciate, either before or now. For the moment, I feel that we must

75

all accept that the natural laws and intelligence that prevail in that of which we are aware, are just part of an infinite intelligence. How, then, can you and I pray to something beyond our comprehension?

My friends Myers and Barrett satisfactorily proved that telepathy is a reality - prayers are thoughts. Whenever you pray to God, your thoughts are heard by those who have chosen to be concerned with your welfare. The quality of your prayer determines the level of consciousness it reaches. Not every person is aware of their invisible guardians and so it is generally accepted that mankind prays to God. The forces that make absent healing possible are the same as those in prayer. Your guardians know of your needs. Prayers are often prayers of want that do not coincide with those needs, that is why many prayers would seem to be unanswered.

The group assembled here are aware of the requests (prayers) made by the medium. If we are able to help and his requests fit his needs, then it is our pleasure to answer his prayers. Should his thoughts deserve greater understanding than we can give, then they penetrate levels of mind higher than ours until they reach that level befitting their quality. Therefore, I assure you that your prayers are heard by those who do God's work. Ask for that which enhances your spiritual progress and you will receive - prayer is necessary.

As for God's will being done on earth as it is in heaven - heaven obviously refers to those higher levels of mind where knowledge, wisdom and love reign. This section of "The Lord's Prayer" is a hope that, one day, these qualities will replace the ignorance, superstition, jealousy and greed that still seem to plague mankind. In the same prayer, it is suggested that God's will exists in heaven. Once again, if heaven relates to those higher levels of mind, then no doubt God's will - love - does dominate those realms. If heaven simply refers to the invisible world in general, then one must take into consideration the lower levels of mind that equate to the more sordid conditions of earthly life. I do feel that, if all the requests contained within "The Lord's Prayer" were answered, then there would no longer be a need for man to continue the trials of physical life.

As I have stated, prayer is thought. Thought is a transmission of energy through the ether. This being so, prayer may be directed from your mind to others on earth, or to God, through the intermediary of those invisible friends who try to guide you. In a sense, we also pray to those who dwell in higher states of consciousness. If many minds transmit the same thought, then the strength of the

76

prayer is in proportion to the number of minds transmitting or praying. I, therefore, pray that you in your prayers would seek knowledge, understanding and wisdom from those in higher vibrations of mind than yourself. As we turn our thoughts to healing, I urge you to also pray or direct your thoughts to those around you, for your thoughts are powerful carriers of healing energy.

HEALING

When living in physical form, I used to accompany several ladies in order to give healing to those who suffered either physically or mentally. I must confess that, in those days, I knew less about the mechanics of this phenomenon than I now know. Let me, then, try to give you thoughts on this, perhaps the greatest of all gifts. My good friend Franz postulated the theory that a magnetic fluid flowed from him to his patients. He also used magnets, sometimes in the shape of human organs. His methods were later ridiculed by the medical men of his time yet, the percentage of successful cures was as high and maybe higher than that of today, no matter which method is employed. It was only the wording that was incorrect, for electromagnetic forces do flow from all who involve themselves in the practice of healing, providing they have that necessary empathy for their patients. Armand Jacques Marie Chasenet (known as Phillippe) wrote a book entitled "Magnetisme Animal". He is one of our group and, therefore, it is befitting that we make comment on this type of healing first. Although there are seven auras, for the purpose of discussing the healing process, let us condense these into three - the physical, mental and spiritual.

The physical body contains a network of electromagnetic circuits that may be seen as seven integrated patterns all linked together. Acupuncturists work with knowledge of these centres of energy. Just as a magnetised piece of steel is surrounded by a beautiful force field, so it is with those seven centres of energy. Together they form a very complex field of magnetism, colour and radiation, known as the physical aura. It may be photographed in the light of a high voltage spark and some sensitives can even see this aura by using their clear-seeing (clairvoyance). Those who have made a study of the delicate patterns and colours can see where lies the origin of any health problems. Some who use pendulums are able to dowse the many lay lines and megaliths of the human body and, from their work, know which of the circuits have ceased to function.

77

Clairsentients become sensitive to that part of the body that requires healing. The vital body forms part of this physical aura and healers whose vitality is high may allow some of theirs to flow to the aura of their patient. In science, it is well known that in a "U" tube containing water, the water in both legs will find its own level. Since the mind is linked through the etheric body to the physical, the amount of energy flow is controlled by the mind. This energy is not only in the form of minute electromagnetic charges, but also contains other etheric vibrations including heat, colour and other radiations. Here it is interesting to note that an infinite number of steel needles may be magnetised from a permanent magnet without it losing any of its magnetic strength. This is achieved by the action of stroking the needles several times in the same direction. Similarly, the hands of the healer make passes in the same direction, working from the part of the body that needs healing to the nearest extremity. A book could be written on just this one aspect of healing, but suffice it here for me to mention that this form of healing includes the use of colour, crystals and knowledge of where, on the hands, feet and head lie the harmonic vibrations of the seven energy centres.

With regard to colour, healers should be aware that the seven basic colours from red to violet correspond to those centres that are to-day called chakras. Depending upon the location of the complaint, the healer should have vision of the appropriate colour when making passes, or even in just the laying on of hands. The use of crystals of various colours act rather similarly to condensers in electrical circuits; in other words, they hold a charge of the vibrations associated with that particular colour. Because they are crystal, they may be compared with gem stones that have gathered earth energy over many, many years. The same principle is involved when you stand with your back against a mature tree, so that you may absorb some of the tree's natural energy. As a healer, it is easier to carry crystals than to take your patients to a large oak tree.

Before discussing other categories of healing, it must be said that even the administration of powerful healing vibrations will not change the time of physical death if a person is meant to leave earthly conditions. When healing involved body, mind and soul, then although the body may not be meant to recover, at least mind and soul are prepared for that inevitable journey. This statement leads us into other forms of healing.

"They only had to touch the hem of his garment and they were healed". If this biblical quotation is true, then was it the vibrations that issued from that garment, or was it the faith that people had in the Nazarene? Experiments have been conducted using sweetened, coloured water instead of medicinal drugs and many patients have responded to this placebo phenomenon - "Faith can move mountains". The power of the mind is so great that it can work on the etheric body with such great effect that the physical body has no choice but to follow suit. Although acupuncture, aromatherapy, reflexology and other similar alternative therapies all have their place, who can say whether the cure is as a result of their administration or due to the faith of the patient in those sciences? Hypnotherapy, when used in competent hands proves that the mind may overcome many maladies of the physical body. The mind, superior to any radio transmitter, may transmit etheric parts of the five physical senses. It may also transmit mannerisms, memories, emotions and guidance, as displayed in mediumship. As well as all these forces, the mind may also transmit radioactive healing energies from the level of consciousness to which it belongs. This applies to mind whether incarnate or discarnate and, therefore, has great implications for those who desire to develop that wonderful gift of healing.

"Physician, heal thyself". This surely implies that every incarnate being has the ability to practice self-healing, provided they know how to direct their mind in order to achieve the desired result. It also implies that those who practice healing should be on a high level of consciousness so that they may utilise the energies of that level with maximum effect. Every healer should also have qualities within their personalities that radiate confidence to those who come to them for help. Those healers who have knowledge of these facts can also help their patients to have a positive attitude and teach them how to use their own minds to have the desired effect on their physical bodies. Just as the earthly sun radiates invisible light that may be split by a prism into seven basic frequencies, a similar process exists in invisible dimensions. The non-physical light of each level of consciousness may be divided into infinite colours with their hues and shades. The mind of the healer can pass these energies into the energy centres of their patients via the etheric body. You are all spiritual beings and therefore this type of healing may rightly be called "Spiritual Healing". If its administration helps the mind and body, then it also helps the soul or spirit of the recipient. I often say that I do not like the terminology of "Spirit World", for it seems to suggest that our world is like a distant planet when, in fact it is, in a sense, only a higher vibrational frequency of earthly conditions. In the same way, those in our world who participate in helping incarnate healers simply use their minds to add energy to that upon which you draw. Helpers in our world must be on a similar level to those with whom they work in yours. Naturally, many "spirit" helpers were involved in curing the sick when they lived on earth. Just as I still try to help many with their scientific work, so doctors, nurses and other caring souls continue their interest here in our dimensions.

Healing on earth implies trying to help others in your dimension, but healing in our levels has even greater meaning. Although after physical death there is no body to heal, the etheric double of many requires help. There are those who enter levels of mind here who do not accept that they have now lost their earthly body. This being so, their etheric still suffers in the same way as their physical body suffered when living on earth. Healing is therefore necessary in our world as well as yours, to help these souls rectify the problems of the etheric body. This is achieved by giving enlightenment, knowledge and truth. Healers on earth can give the same to their patients, so that, although the physical body cannot always be completely restored, at least people are aware that poverty of bodily health often helps the mind and soul to become rich in wisdom. All learning is painful in the sense that it stretches the mind. Learning gives knowledge. Knowledge encourages experience. Experience eventually gives wisdom and wisdom gives greater luminosity to the soul. In your healing, try to help others to see that earthly life is but one of God's many nursery schools and that the time spent in this nursery school is a mere nothing compared to eternity.

Accept also that this learning process, of necessity, involves Karma. An athlete cannot become a world champion without practice and training of the muscles of his body. This involves discipline and often pain. Likewise, a soul may not become a master, unless it undergoes the necessary mental and spiritual development. How can we learn to love that great, incomprehensible, infinite source of creation unless we first learn to love our parents, brothers, relations and even friends? How many can truly say that they love their neighbours as much as they love themselves? Could it be that, before understanding poverty, one has to suffer it? Before understanding the many afflictions of the physical body it is surely necessary to experience at least some of these earthly handicaps. An understanding of all these tools of knowledge are necessary for the healer to do his work. Comments on Karma deserve a separate chapter and, therefore let us try to give some sense to the reality of this subject, since it not only applies to the human species, but to all kingdoms whether animate or inanimate.

Karma, Astrology and Ancestry

Chapter 8

KARMA, ASTROLOGY AND ANCESTRY

In previous chapters, I have suggested that the infancy of mind lies in the law and order that prevail even in one atom and that it is possible to see, in higher states of existence, that this elementary mind gradually becomes more and more sophisticated. Allow me to stretch your mind by asking one or two questions and then endeavouring to give some sensible answers. Is the one life of a daisy sufficient for the mind force of that daisy to move on to a higher form of manifestation, or should that mind first suffer drought, floods, fertile and infertile ground? The hardships and trials of these conditions of nature would surely strengthen that mind, making it more ready for the trials of a greater challenge. How is this achieved? The mind of that particular daisy returns to one of those infinite plant and vegetable levels; the level is determined by natural forces and experience, thus helping that level to rise a little higher. That same non-individualised mind of the daisy does not bemoan the conditions of its earthly life, but accepts them as necessary experiences for its level of mind. How many people accept the conditions of their life in the same manner?

Extremes of conditions must exist in all manifestations of life so that mind can observe them and, from observation, learn. Mankind is only aware of blindness, cruelty, disease, deformity, poverty and riches because these factors exist in his world. Without them, mind could not learn, could not gain experience and would never progress. As the mind of mankind has become individualised, naturally each individual must learn by the physical experiences that life presents. One cannot understand poverty of the spirit unless one has first experienced earthly poverty. Once again, I remind you that the thoughts expressed on these matters are not only my thoughts but include teachings from those wiser than myself. From what I am told, the mind must benefit from the variety of experiences afforded by earthly incarnation and the vastness of these physical challenges may not be experienced in one lifetime. As I mentioned in the chapter on reincarnation, there comes a time when one has mastered earthly trials, sufficient to stay in the mind world where experiences of a different nature exist. It would seem that, by natural laws, the misgivings of one life must be paid for in another. Also, the knowledge, experience and wisdom that one gathers in the harvest of earthly journeys must be shared with others who are incarnate. This can only be achieved by returning to the world of matter or, alternatively, trying telepathically to influence the minds of those on earth. Always, there is freedom of choice and one may postpone a Karmic necessity until the individual feels ready to return. Thus, many realise that more earthly trials will remove the stumbling blocks of spiritual progression and enfoldment, whilst others realise that physical incarnation is necessary to teach those who are deaf to the thoughts transmitted from our world. The moral behind this is surely to learn and experience as many lessons as possible whilst incarnate, so that the vibrations of your mind and spirit need no longer be tied by a silver cord to another earthly vehicle.

You probably wonder why I feel that there is a link between Karma, astrology and ancestry. Astrology is based upon the principle that, at the time of birth, the vibrational energy from the heavenly bodies in this solar system have an effect upon the individual. The sun's radiations certainly have a great effect upon many forms of life. The closeness of the moon has a gravitational pull on earth's seas. Magnetic lines of force affect earthly objects, the force of those objects, as well as the closeness or proximity. Without giving further examples, it is not unreasonable to suggest that, as a new-born baby emerges from the protection of the mother's body, it too is affected by the vibrations emitted from all the same forces in this solar system; the closer the planet in position at the time of birth, the greater the effect. There can be no doubt that those born under the same zodiac sign have similar characteristics within their personalities. In similar fashion, those born on similar latitudes, longitudes, countries, towns and villages are affected by them. Combining all of these features gives birth to the science of astrology. In our opinion, these vibrations and forces also present a Karmic challenge. I do not have the knowledge to go into the finer aspects of astrology yet, at the same time, suggest that each sign of the zodiac presents different challenges to the individual. To be more precise, those who benefit from the natural leadership qualities of the Leo, must learn to use those qualities to help others without becoming domineering, aggressive or selfish. Even the lion can be tamed.

Let us now consider ancestry, for there can be no doubt that the body in which the spirit and mind manifest is determined by genealogy, including such patterns as those laid down by D.N.A. molecules, etc. In the same way as I suggested the body is affected by cosmic vibrations, so the physical qualities, or lack of them, is influenced by one's ancestors. It certainly seems that certain diseases or complaints are hereditary. Even sensitivity and mediumship seem to follow a similar pattern, in the sense that children of psychically gifted people often inherit the same gifts. How can we explain this?

I have already endeavoured to define the differentiation between spirit, mind, etheric and body. It is also generally accepted that the physical brain has two hemispheres, the left affording the ability to express physical and material aspects of the mind, whilst the right hemisphere provides a facility for such facets as intuition, emotion and love. The genes that make up the body are part of one's ancestral chain and, therefore, determine many factors in the vehicle that mind and spirit control. It could, therefore, be said that ancestry presents a challenge for mind and spirit. Even the length of physical incarnation can be affected by the behaviour of these minute building blocks of the physical body. If all human bodies were exactly the same, then many Karmic lessons could not be learnt. These building blocks also pass through evolution and become more proficient with each generation. Man now runs faster, jumps higher and is greatly improved when compared physically to his ancestors. As mind and spirit evolve, so it is necessary for the earthly vehicles they control to progress proportionally. The elemental and vital mind that influences each gene and particle of the physical body belong to the same Karmic journey that all manifestations of life follow.

We here, although individual, are part of a group. That group is one of an infinite number that constitute the level of consciousness in which we dwell. That level is but one level within the sphere to which we presently belong and that sphere is one of seven in this minute part of creation. No doubt those seven spheres are like one atom within the infinity of creation. Similarly, those small particles of which your body consists are part of the great you.

The spirit uses mind to influence the etheric and thus the physical body. The progress of spirit depends upon the development of mind, which in turn depends upon the challenges afforded by the physical body. I maintain that these challenges are brought about by the vibrational influences of this solar system, as well as the genetic construction of the body in which the spirit manifests during its Karmic struggle in the university of physical life. Perhaps you can now accept a relationship between Karma, astrology and ancestry.

Kingdoms of Life

Chapter 9

THE KINGDOMS OF LIFE

In all the preceding chapters, I have re-postulated in a more simplistic fashion many of the ideas that I expressed in the past. Death does not give all the secrets and mysteries of God's creation. Only as the mind develops is it capable of understanding the imponderables of matter, life and spirit, and the group of which I am part consists of students in the university of life. Physical death simply removes the handicaps of the five senses, giving the student greater freedom to progress in learning. I have already stated that matter is ether in a low state of vibration - a condensation of the invisible into the visible. Animated matter is no different than the inanimate, except that life manifests itself in association with such an organism. In the inorganic, matter exists in the form of solids, liquids and gases; matter also exists in the form of complex molecules called protoplasm that forms the vehicle for life in its many forms. But what is this stuff called life? When it forms a relationship with matter it has a character and identity of its own. Life is mind in its many stages, temporarily joined to matter for the purpose of striving towards perfection. Mind is ether in a higher frequency than that used by light, electricity, magnetism and other forces. At the moment of conception, there is a spiritual magnetic attraction from the new vehicle to that level of mind suitable for life to manifest. Remember that mind exists in both low and high orders, in non-individualised and individualised forms. It would not be natural for your mind to be joined to the body of an amoeba, nor for that amoebic level of mind to dwell in human form. In earthly conditions it may appear that mistakes are sometimes made, for highly developed minds sometimes dwell in limited protoplasmic conditions, and vice versa. Forgive my rather dry sense of humour.

In the lower kingdoms of life such as the plant and vegetable, the mind that joins its protoplasmic vehicle is of such low order that, at physical death, it releases also the etheric double and returns to its appropriate level. As we move up the scale of life manifestation, mind clings hold of the etheric for a period of time. This time varies according to the type of species. Even the mind of an ant has not developed consciousness sufficient to hold on to its etheric counterpart, whereas the higher orders of the animal world can retain their etheric existence for a while. If certain animals have received love, affection and care, then they can stay in etheric form for as long as necessary. This accounts for the fact that our pets are often there to greet us when we cross that border-land between visible and invisible worlds. On planet earth, it would seem that man has just about developed his mind and self consciousness enough to be able to retain the etheric, thus enabling him to be an individual personality until he progresses far enough to put aside the necessity of shape and form. At this stage he will become just light - a spiritual photonic part of that which we call God. This, for the moment, is beyond both your and our comprehension.

When discussing life, it is natural that man only refers to that which appeals to his senses and, therefore, with regard to kingdoms, we should start with that which is termed mineral - the inorganic according to definition - yet even in one single atom there appears to be some law and order of low degree. It could be said that, even here, there are vibrations within the ether sufficient to allow the very existence of that atom. In a sense, mind manifests even within a single atom, but in such a low form as only to require that atom to combine with others to form molecules and, hence, the chemical elements of matter that constitute the mineral kingdom. In the evolution of this solar system, the stage had to be set before the play of life could begin. By the processes of the mother part of God, nature then set the scenery, utilising the etheric vibrations emitted by the sun, moon, planets and other forces such as magnetism, electricity, gravity and cohesion. Thus the earth was void apart from these etheric vibrations. Higher mind then exerted its influence on the vibrations within the mineral kingdom causing elements to combine. The law and order that persisted in these combinations caused vibrations of a higher nature that could be called life force or the birth of mind in very low form. The difference resulted in the necessity for locomotion and expansion. Coral and sponges formed amongst many other primeval forms of life and, as mind expanded, the desire to propagate species took place. To be more explicit, the combination of certain elements caused a natural attraction of mind in its lowest form that is termed "life force".

Mind has an inborn desire to expand, making use of all available etheric vibrations. No doubt the first sign of life was a virus within the ocean, takings its nourishment from the many chemicals dissolved in the water. Some of the viruses would take the necessities of life from the bed of those oceans; they would cling to the ground and, by taking different elements of food, would form the first plant life. Eventually, some of the free viruses would expand, forming single cell organisms. In some of these organisms, the expansion of mind brought about the development of fish. From this, it is easy to see how life gradually manifested on land. By the process of evolution from fish to reptile, to animal, to man, mind continued to expand until it was capable of retaining sufficient etheric viscosity to remain individualised. When this stage was reached, mind could survive in individual particles even independently of its earthly vehicle. This hypothesis is just as sensible as that formed by religious authorities who suggested that some supreme being spoke the word and it was so. In our level of consciousness, we can only suggest how we came to be. We are no nearer to a conception of God and creation than we were when living in earthly conditions. We, like you, can only say "I am", and describe the conditions in which we find ourselves. Not all reptiles crept onto land to form animals. That great architect of creation saw that it was necessary to leave a blueprint of design so that our minds could be stimulated into pondering both our origin and destiny.

I vaguely remember writing books, one of which postulated my thoughts, at the time, on life and matter. It is my hope that readers may better understand these thoughts as I now expand on them. Certain chemical elements such as carbon and water have remarkable properties of attracting other elements and combining with them. This is part of the law and order that persisted when earth had cooled sufficiently to allow their existence. Mind, in very low degree, was manifest even in those first condensations of ether known as atoms, chemical elements and matter. That form of mind we term law and order. As chemical elements combined with acids, the vibrations of that law and order increased until the day arrived when that vibration demanded locomotion. At this stage, the form of mind could be termed life force and as this life force expanded in the development of species, so that life force could then be called mind. When the vibration of mind increased to such a stage as to desire and attain individualism, then those vibrations were termed spirit. Yet all the vibrations are simply ether in different energy manifestations.

The blueprints of all kingdoms still exist today - the mineral, plant and vegetable, animal and human kingdoms - all there to show how body and mind have developed on a parallel course. This hypothesis suggests that your minds have within them experiences gained in all these kingdoms.

Just as we in another kingdom are still concerned with those kingdoms through which we have passed, maybe man should be more concerned with those kingdoms that lie below him. My son Raymond joins me again, to help stimulate your thoughts on these matters:-

As I raise my thoughts to God on high
I ask why in his creation he included the fly
For flies caused great annoyance to me,
Yet the spider ate them with very great glee.
The birds, in turn, loved that spider to eat
Instead of seed it was for them a treat.
Our cat did try hard to find that bird,
Was this all meant, or is it absurd?
Where does this end I ask myself
As I reach for tinned meat just on my shelf.
The answer seemed to come from above
God provides for all with his great love.
All the kingdoms are linked together
So that souls may continue for ever
To climb through all those levels of mind
All of them trying their destiny to find.
Before the next fly I try to kill
I'll remember it's here simply by God's will.
As I eat that meat, should I feel shame
Or just give thanks to from whence it came.

In that great scheme of creation, it seems that creatures in those lower kingdoms expect their end as a step forward in the evolution of mind to which they belong. Although the law of self-preservation prevails, they do not seem to have the same fear of death as does the mind of man. Maybe the sub-consciousness of eternity lies nearer to the surface of their level of mind than it does in mankind. Those in the lower levels no doubt feel that those in the next kingdom are Gods, just as those in ancient days thought the voices they heard were the voice of God. At least, some are now willing to listen and understand that we, in the invisible world, are only one kingdom higher. We are not Gods, neither are they who dwell in still higher kingdoms. In my ignorance, I feel that creation is forever expanding and that, therefore, God will be eternally beyond our reach. If that which we understand as God was within our mind's reach, infinity or eternity could not exist. Those who claim to have seen God, Jesus or

90

other great souls have simply seen their mentor, who wisely takes on the guise of that great spirit that they expect to see. Ask and ye shall receive contains a greater philosophy than mankind appreciates.

Just as the fly does not understand the kingdom of the birds or fish, neither do we understand that sphere of spirit that lies ahead of us. We may be given a glimpse of the next level of consciousness within our sphere but, as for that next sphere, it is as much beyond our comprehension as our sphere is to your earthly vibrations. The larva cannot appreciate the world of the fly until it is born into that world. The caterpillar likewise does not appreciate the butterfly world. The astral world does not appreciate the mental spheres; neither do those in mental spheres appreciate those spheres termed celestial or divine. Do not, therefore, ask us to inform you of the ultimate to progression beyond these seven invisible spheres, for we are only yet infants in that sphere and level in which we find ourselves. I cannot, therefore, continue to write about that of which I and my friends have no knowledge. Those who have this wisdom reside in vibrations that are far above both our and your ken.

Thus it is that infinite mind sees the necessity for the kingdoms of mineral, plant and vegetable, animal and human in this part of creation yet, within each of these kingdoms, we see a vast variety of species. Even within the mineral kingdom there are all the chemical elements with their multitudinous combinations in the forms of solid, liquid and gas. No doubt the law and order that prevails in simple sandstone is of a lower order than that within a precious crystal or gemstone and, in a sense, there is a reincarnation of this law and order as we move from one species of mineral to another. See, also, the great variety of life force within the plant world as we move from a simple blade of grass to the Venus Fly-catching plant. In the animal world we see the same variety of species ranging from the mouse to the ape. It is not surprising that within humanity we find some whose mind is of very low order and others whom we describe as genius. At this stage of mind development, it is no longer necessary to have the same variety of vehicles as that in the insect, fish and bird worlds. When individuality has been achieved, it would seem that differences in skin colour and stature are sufficient for the progression of human spirit, until the time comes when even a physical vehicle is no longer required and that etheric umbilical cord is severed for ever.

Here we may draw a parallel to our invisible world for, as we have stated, within each sphere or invisible kingdom there are an infinite number of levels or species of consciousness. Each one of us here, although individual, are atoms or parts of the whole level of mind in which we exist. That level is, in turn, just one part of the sphere to which it belongs and that sphere is just one of the seven in this microscopic part of creation. Common sense suggests that the seven spheres are yet one very small part of a greater whole - ad infinitum. If we could comprehend this infinite chain of mind progression then, in its totality, it would surely constitute what we call God.

Each cell of your body is quite happy to belong to one of the seven energy centres that constitute your whole, with its many subdivisions of organs and systems. I suggest that mankind has not yet reached that stage when he is quite happy to be part of a greater whole. For the moment, he seems as if he wants to be king within his own kingdom, having very little thought for the existence of others.

Mediumship

Chapter 10

MEDIUMSHIP

My friends Barrett and Myers demonstrated sufficiently that an idea, a picture or a sensation could be transmitted from one mind to another. I refer to those experiments of sensory perception by telepathic means. At no time did they ever demonstrate that sentences, paragraphs or books could be passed from one mind to another, although I must confess that Myers has occasionally managed to get a Latin phrase through the mediumship of Mrs. Leonard. I do feel it important for mediums to realise that the language of the mind is vastly different to earthly language. We in the mind world may only transmit pictures, feelings and ideas to one another and to those on earth whose mind frequency is similar. How many of you can hold a communication with a friend without using any organs or parts of your physical body? Certainly in conscious state, the five physical senses are a handicap to mental telepathy. Just as a blind person can usually hear, feel and smell more easily than those who can see, so we without any physical handicaps, find that the sixth, seventh and higher senses function far better in invisible dimensions than when living in a physical environment. It is obvious from the animals, birds, fish and even insects, that when the language of sound is limited, the language of the mind is accentuated. So it is in my world. I can communicate with those in my level of consciousness without even uttering a word.

No doubt, in the visible world, those in one level of consciousness find it hard to communicate with those in another. Only with patience, time, perseverance and love will you ever be able to communicate with your pets and, even then, communication has its limitations. See, then, our difficulty in trying to impress the mind of this sensitive to use the correct earthly words that describe our thoughts, feelings and ideas. The more passive the conscious mind of the medium the easier it is to convey thoughts from our world to yours. Even when the sensitive is in very deep trance, we must still use mind language. I often marvel at the fact that we are ever able to make those on earth aware of our invisible world.

Many who claim to see us clairvoyantly do not really see us - only the vision that we can mentally transmit from our mind to theirs, the exception being those rare times when we are able to borrow physical vibrations to dress ourselves - sometimes partially or thinly, other times, fully. Similarly, clairaudients say that they can hear our voices. Once again, their physical ears can only hear us if we are fortunate enough to utilise physical energy so that vibrations in the air affect the diaphragm of the ear. This, of course, takes place in that phenomena called direct voice. Even then, it is still a telepathic process involving mind to mind communication. The thoughts received by the medium pass along an ectoplasmic link to the voice box which vibrates the air, yet the words are the result of the turning of those thoughts into words by the medium's mind. Occasionally, when conditions are very good, the medium chooses a word that exactly matches our thought. In earthly life, there are times when you feel that the telephone will ring and that a certain person's voice will be heard through that instrument. This is called clairsentience and is another method of telepathically transmitting a feeling. So far, I have tried to describe the mechanics of mediumship in the form of clairvoyance, clairaudience and clairsentience. Let us try to give similar explanations to all the other forms of mediumship.

Many great composers, artists, musicians, actors, scientists and others who aspire to develop some art of expression are inspired from our levels. Those who have chosen to be your spiritual guardians, know your needs and bring appropriate helpers, who try to feed your mind with advice and ideas. This type of mediumship exists with all people who thirst for knowledge. Without wishing to sound too biblical, ask and ye shall receive, but only that which is necessary for your spiritual education. The converse equally applies in the fact that those who do not ask obviously feel that they do not, for the moment, need help. These souls are never deserted, but natural laws come into play so that, eventually, a time comes in their lives when a cry for help is heard.

Sensitive people are able to put aside thoughts of a material or physical nature, thus enabling them to receive full benefit from their inspirers. Some are even able to take both hands off their bodily vehicle so that a driver from an invisible dimension may have full control. This is known as deep trance mediumship, in which some external mind has the temporary facilities of the physical brain and body of the medium. Even this has its limitations, since the physical brain of the medium is a different computer than that previously used in life by the communicating mind. Trance mediumship may vary from just slight inspiration to the ability of the spirit to give to the medium complete ideas, visions, feelings and mannerisms. In very deep trance mediumship it is often necessary for there to be a team of invisible friends all playing their parts in the telepathic transmission. In this particular case it is Phillippe who injects the necessary more feminine, delicate vibrations to compensate for the more logical, scientific personality of our medium. Franz is totally responsible for arranging the state of unconsciousness, so that I and others may pass our thoughts through a reasonably unrestricted channel.

In clairvoyance, clairaudience, clairsentience and even trance, there is no guarantee or necessity for intervention from our world. Let me clarify this. Your earthly companions are mind, just as capable as ours. They too can transmit visions, ideas and feelings to sensitive receivers in either conscious or unconscious state. It is therefore necessary to try to differentiate between incarnate and discarnate mind instead of assuming that all communication comes from "the Spirit World". Only patient research or biblically testing the spirit will help to determine the origin of the telepathic transmission. As I remember my meetings with Mrs. Piper, I am prompted (maybe inspired) to mention automatic writing. Sometimes this medium would enter an unconscious deep trance when communicators would, through her guide, use the facilities of her voice. On other occasions, the medium would enter a semi-conscious state, in which her hand would be used to write the thoughts of those who transmitted them. In both trance and automatic writing, the secondary personality need not be obtrusive or troublesome; it is well controlled and amenable to reason, but it is not the normal intelligence of the medium. Here it should be mentioned that those who, because of their low level of mind, allow visitors from our lower spheres to influence them, often find such influences both unreasonable and obtrusive. This is also mediumship, but better termed "possession".

We are, at present, passing thoughts with regard to mental mediumship in the form of mind to mind communication without the utilisation of any physical energy. These thoughts can be in the form of evidence, when memories of those in invisible realms are able to reach someone who has knowledge of their life on earth. At other times, the transmission of thought is in the form of knowledge, wisdom and philosophy beyond the normal capability of the medium. I am aware that music, poetry, artistic feelings and scientific ideas are all passed from our world to yours and, therefore, mediumship means much more than the link between members of an earthly family. Every person on earth who asks help from our realms so that they may help other earthly friends acts as a medium.

This desire to help others stands out more in the mediumship of healing. We have already given some information on this particular gift, but allow us to add to it. Your mind is you. You are not your body. The mind determines what every cell in your body should do and uses the semi-physical etheric substance to achieve this. By directing or focusing your thoughts on the physical welfare of others, you may often help them to heal themselves. We have also stated that if we could guarantee the effectiveness of our transmissions of thought, then there would be no physical or mental illness in your world. Those in our world who concern themselves about the bodily and mental health of friends on earth, need a medium who can channel not only thoughts but cosmic healing radiations from our worlds to yours. In scientific terms, they could well be called an intermediate frequency. We have, in previous chapters, stated that the light of our levels may be transmitted to those whose mediumship is in the form of healing, yet this gift may also manifest in a physical phenomenon. Not all physical mediums use ectoplasm to form materialisations or to transfigure the medium's features. Some healers have sufficient physical energy to enable them to de-materialise diseased parts of the body. Others can use this same energy to perform a similar operation to earthly surgeons, but with one great difference; any external or internal incisions heal immediately, by the combination of physical ectoplasm and vibrations from our world. The mediumship of healing is therefore both physical and mental phenomena.

I often regretted the fact that, when in earthly conditions, I did not accept invitations from my good friend William Crookes to witness the phenomena displayed by that powerful medium Daniel Dunglas Home. Eusapia Palladino did have a similar gift, but could only produce the phenomena in more subdued light. The mediumship to which I now refer is that called "physical mediumship", which embraces the phenomena of materialisation, direct voice, movement of objects and levitation, as well as other strange phenomena.

In this chapter, I only wish to mention the fact that mediumship occurs in both mental and physical forms and that I was privileged to witness both. Other books relate details of these phenomena and, therefore, I feel it would be unnecessary to repeat that which has already been described. However, in the light of our present knowledge, we as a group feel it important to stress that, due to the limitations of available energy, more truth, philosophy, knowledge and wisdom can be transmitted in mental mediumship than in physical.

We also know that the great teachers of both past and present only displayed physical phenomena to make mankind realise that there were forces that did not belong to earthly sciences. Unfortunately, this state of mind still prevails today so that, before a medium can command attention of the many, they have first to produce some spectacular physical phenomena. Nobody wants to listen - and yet. Both mental and physical phenomena are still necessary, but do not expect one medium to have both developed to a very high standard. Although there are always exceptions, generally to one is given the gift of knowledge and wisdom; to another is given the gift of allowing invisible friends to mould the ectoplasmic energy that is emitted from their natural bodily orifices. It is a desire of the invisible world that, in time, sufficient phenomena and evidence will have been given so that more emphasis will be placed on listening and learning, rather than just seeing and hearing. Remember that it is possible to hear without listening, but learning requires the ability of the mind to listen.

Mediumship is like a diamond with its many facets. Those who have allowed one of those facets to develop have a glistening light that they may show others the way. It could also be compared with a wheel that has many spokes, all leading to the centre of its being. So far we have only made reference to the spokes of clairvoyance, clairaudience, trance, healing and some forms of physical mediumship. Let us try to throw some light on the mechanics of other forms of physical mediumship. Let us try to throw some light on the mechanics of other forms of communication between our world and yours. Before doing this, however, allow us to stress one point. The students in the university of life must learn to differentiate between psychic and mediumistic abilities.

The human body is a shadow of the real self - the mind - in the fact that we are all like snowflakes, each with its different pattern. The lines on the hands, the fingerprints, the auras, the numbers and colours associated with names, the birth time and places, the shape of heads and fingers are all part of one's spiritual shadow. Those who apply themselves to the study of these parts are able to give some indication of the real self. The experts may make it appear that the information is being relayed from the invisible world, when in truth they are simply giving a meaning to that which they perceive. This is not an attempt to belittle such abilities, but only once again to stress the difference between the psychic and the medium. It is possible for some earthly individuals to use their mind so that an image can appear on photographic paper. They can even determine the nature of that image without any assistance from invisible friends. On the other hand, there are others who can supply the necessary energy for some in our dimension to place an image of themselves on that light-sensitive paper. Mind can influence vibrations within the ether, whether that mind be incarnate or discarnate. Here I refer to those who have the mediumship enabling "Spirit Photography" to manifest. In a similar manner, some here can influence radio-like waves, so that voice imprints are made on earthly magnetic iron-oxide plastic tapes. These various phenomena are all produced by mind being able to interfere with the lower vibrations or frequencies within the etheric wave band. There are minds in our levels who can influence the gravitational frequencies and thus produce the phenomenon of levitation. My friend William Crookes showed me a "spirit photograph" of his dear wife. In all these various phenomena it is necessary to employ the physical energies that surround some earthly being - the medium.

If the science of psychometry is a reality, then the vibrations of every object and person that you have touched must lie within your auric emanations. A very sensitive person can become aware of these vibrations without any intervention from invisible dimensions. A medium is able to give information that is not contained within any bodily or auric fields of energy and, of necessity, must receive that information telepathically from some external source.

A sensitive, or psychic person is, then, one who is able to become aware of patterns and vibrations transmitted from your physical body - the shadow of your mind. A medium is a person who can become aware of external minds and relay information by either mental or physical means. All this makes the task of research and conclusion very difficult, although those who understand these facts are far better equipped to prove the survival of human personality. To digress for one moment. I have attempted to` influence the mind of this medium to read that book entitled "Human Personality" written by my friend Myers, but so far he has not obtained it, nor really tried. An understanding of all facets of psychic abilities and mediumistic gifts is necessary before one can collect evidence from the wealth of phenomena that exists to-day. It may seem that physical mediums able to produce materialisations are not as prevalent as in my day, but think for a moment of all the additional evidence that has taken its place. All the mental and physical mediumship of the past has not rid the world of war, torture, jealousy, greed and selfishness. As our mentor would say "Earth is full of God's beauty and love, yet most of mankind is too blind and insensitive to appreciate it". A favourite expression of this medium's father is "Cannot see the wood for the trees".

Unexplained objects appear in your skies. Egyptian hieroglyphic patterns manifest in cornfields and deserts. Voices and images seem to manifest on your modern technological instruments. Yet, as in the past, nobody wants to see, nobody wants to listen - and yet. Even modern scientists tell of the strange behaviour of sub-atomic particles. Mathematicians suggest that there is scientific proof of parallel invisible universes. Many are able, more than ever, to report exteriorising out of their physical bodies. A great teacher repeats similar miracles to those who preceded him. All these phenomena and more, yet, as I read the brain pattern of Raymond, this medium, it would appear that explanations for some of these strange, mystical phenomena are: hedgehogs mating and aviation improvements, etc. etc. - ridiculous. In all these things - first study, to gather knowledge. Add experience to that knowledge. With these two come wisdom and, gradually, an understanding of God's reason for creation - infinite love.

In all the multifarious mediumship that exists, we feel that the more the etheric umbilical cord stretches, the more powerful the mediumship. During inspiration, the etheric is slightly out of co-incidence with the physical body and this state could be compared with day-dreaming. In very deep trance state, the silver cord stretches so that the soul energy has only slight effect on the physical body. Naturally, the nearer to our vibrations the mind of the medium, the easier it is for us to communicate mind to mind. In everyday consciousness, it is just as if the mind were shielded by all the five physical senses.

Mediumship functions through the right hemisphere of the physical brain. The greater the development of this hemisphere, the more potential for the development of one of those many facets of the diamond of mediumship. Those who have this potential have no doubt received it through heredity and, therefore, not only the sins of the fathers, but also the gifts, manifest in the sons and daughters.

There does seem to be a greater prevalence of mediumship in women than in men. Those in my group would suggest that the female of the species has a greater leaning toward development of the right hemisphere, whereas men need greater emphasis on the logical, reasoning, scientific and physical qualities of the left. Without casting any aspersion against the male mediums of both past and present, this, no doubt, accounts for the fact that most male mediums seem to be a little more effeminate than the ordinary man. I would suggest that it is necessary to have experiences using the vehicles of both male and female, so that the many qualities of mind may have an opportunity to expand. In those higher spheres dwell souls who have developed all qualities associated with both sexes and, therefore, their light bears no trace of either male or female. As we try to project our thoughts towards God, we realise that this infinite mind embraces all qualities within father science and mother nature. This does not only apply on this tiny speck of dust - earth - but within the whole of creation, which is for ever expanding. As I stated within the introductory poem in this book, we do not have all the answers. We can only add our thoughts to yours in the light of the experience we have gained in invisible dimensions. In earthly life, the medium needs the qualities of the scientist and those with physical skills, just as they need the insight of the medium.

From all of this it would seem that those with a developed left hemisphere need to develop the right, and vice versa. It also implies that no matter how hard one tries, one may not be able to develop mediumship in this lifetime. One may start by planting the seeds of sensitivity, so that they may grow and flourish in later experiences. In the same way, many mediums would no doubt like to be very skilled in some physical attribute, but will have to wait until an experience presents them with this opportunity. A greater light than mine suggests that mankind must learn to respect the qualities in both male and female, scientist and medium, rich and poor, human and other kingdoms. If this could happen, then the delights of our levels of consciousness would be a little closer to earth. Maybe God's will would and will be done on earth as it is in heaven - in those many mansions.

Thoughts on Religion

Chapter 11

THOUGHTS ON RELIGION

As we draw close to earthly vibrations, it can be clearly seen that churches are losing their influence on people more and more. It is equally true that history reveals that religion has been responsible for more murder, violence, wars and torture than any other organised society. To go into details of these facts would only be a repeat of that which has already been written by my friend Findlay and others. It is sufficient to say that all religions owe their existence to the desire of mankind to understand both his origin and destination; a feeling that the short material life cannot be all and that it must be a prelude to something much finer. The great variety of existing religions cannot all be right, but that is not to say they are all wrong, for most contain a code of conduct which, if followed, guarantees sufficient law and order for the society in which they evolve.

There can be only three possibilities with regards to the thoughts of after life. The utter materialists and many scientists consider that mind and brain are one. They therefore feel that when the body dies, the mind also ceases to exist. Expressing this simply - when your body dies, you die. If this be true, then the thoughts expressed in this book must have their foundations either in Raymond's mind or some earthly mind. Some are a little more lenient in their views and accept the possibility of a universal life force or mind, but without individuality. Many religions still teach that, when the body dies, the soul enters a sleep state until the day of a great resurrection, when all the physical atoms of the body reassemble. Presumably, when that takes place, every human being would once again have physical form and dwell again on this planet earth. Excuse my sense of humour when I suggest that, if we include all that have died in the past, added to all that die in the millennia of years of the future, then the earth may not be large enough physically to support so many. It is no wonder that many scientists do not conform with this idea. The third possibility is, of course, that when the physical body dies, the soul or mind separates as the silver cord is severed. When this occurs, that individualised life force gravitates to a level that befits it. Once again, scientific minds have, in the past, found it difficult to subscribe to this idea, since there were no physical scientific instruments capable of measuring these facts. Sensitives and mediums were burnt at the stake or shut away in asylums. Only in recent times have modern scientists begun to discover the existence of forces and particles that lie outside the laws of earthly physics. It is the desire and work of the group assembled here to try to blend religion and science, for superstition still prevails in both.

Even in our world, there are levels of consciousness in which the inhabitants still adhere to earthly religious thoughts. They still hold church services and feel that their particular religious leader is the true representative of God. Man does survive death and many who have come home, saints and great men, those who have died in service to others, still continue their efforts for the progress and elevation of the earthly human race.

There is no point in making further comment on the first two possibilities, since I know the third to be the reality. I survive and, if conditions are satisfactory, can communicate thoughts to those who are willing to listen. The spiritual world is a reality that should be common knowledge to all religions and politicians. At the moment, ecclesiastics hope and pray that our world exists, yet they differ in their conception of the conditions that prevail in those "many mansions". Politicians often pay lip service to all these religions in the hope that ordinary people will respect them for their actions. It is time that all religions combined into one universal philosophy and prayer became an act of contemplation. The universe is that small part of creation of which mankind is aware. Creation is an infinite ocean of life and mind which will survive the birth and death of galaxies. I am now more aware than ever that this is so, for great minds in levels far above mine sometimes inform us that earth is just one temporary nursery school in that great and infinite school of mind-creation. Even if your earth and its solar system one day ceased to exist in its present form, the life and mind attached to it would find other opportunities of manifesting for there are an infinite number of similar nursery schools. The beauty of a bird's feather, an insect's wing, a flower, a tree, a fish and the whole of nature, virtually shout out that a mind far superior to ours was the architect of their existence - yet most are deaf and blind to the wonders and mysteries of that great mind. Science should be considered as a useful tool that helps man understand a little of these mysteries. The physicist tends to ignore living things and the church tends to behave like a composer with no musical instruments that enable us to become aware of the working of this mind.

In the earthly world, religion and politics are the two main organisations that influence life. Religion deals with the future and, generally, politics with the present. Political guidance has encouraged man to explore icy regions, tropical jungles and the seven seas, yet religion has failed in encouraging man to explore our world. It must be admitted that there has been some progress in the fact that mankind no longer worships the gods of the sun, moon, stars and even thunder and lightening, as he once did. Without giving a history lesson of all religions, it is still true today that each particular religion feels that it, alone, holds the key to the gates of heaven. Those who do not subscribe to their thoughts are considered to be of the devil - the mountain goat.

History shows that religion, like nations and scientific theories, have their periods of birth, growth and decay. Those who in the past were followers of Mithro, Zeus, Isis, Osiris and other teachers, still found their place in one of our infinite levels of mind. Many of the great teachers of the past were, like Jesus, classed as saviour Gods. It is now the time for mankind to realise that he is his own saviour. Belief must be replaced by the knowledge that, as you sow, so will you reap. Superstitions in many holy books must be replaced by knowledge, facts and truth. If only man would open his eyes, he would see that around him there is a wealth of phenomena that cannot be explained by physics alone.

Mankind gained superiority over other kingdoms by expanding his mind because he desired to understand his origin and destiny. He has now risen above worshipping idols and, at last, realises that many thoughts expressed within holy books are those of the ancient clergy who, in their pursuit of power, would instil thoughts of only two destinations - heaven or hell. The time has come for the thoughts of those great teachers of the past to be separated from those expressed by the priests of old. Many friends of mine here would have been considered rich when they were in earthly conditions, yet found their heaven more easily than the effort required to get "a camel through the eye of a needle". What is heaven to one may well be hell to another. Those souls who still pursue interests of a more physical and sensual nature would find my heaven a hell. The music of the great composers may give pain to certain levels of mind. The true message of all teachers and religions is "Love your neighbour as yourself". This message cannot have been heard yet, for many in both your and our dimensions have not learned to either love or understand themselves. All religions should therefore become united, in an effort to help to achieve this aim so that, in time to come, love for one another will prevail.

A parallel could be drawn between the many prevailing religions that preach their thoughts to the masses and the infinite levels in our world who try to communicate their thoughts to earthly friends. No incarnate or discarnate being knows the ultimate truth. Those of you who dwell in earthly dimension feel that heaven is a place that is up and hell is a region somewhere below it. We also feel that finer conditions lie somewhere above and grosser conditions below. In other words, in whichever level of mind we find ourselves, we know, instinctively, there prevails both better and worse.

Just as the more orthodox religions have different doctrines, even spiritualism is sub-divided. There are those who would pay greater tribute to the medium Jesus. Others disagree about the theory of reincarnation. I have already stated that those minds that have the answers to such questions dwell in spheres well beyond communicative ability with earthly minds. All religions, including spiritualism, should be proud of the truths they have found, but also humble and penitent for the mistakes and false teachings they have made and given. Instead, they remain arrogant and reactionary, dwelling in temples amidst the degradation, filth, poverty, war and ignorance of mankind. It is no wonder that men of science still hesitate to use the tools of their trade so that all religions could rid themselves of the false doctrines and superstitions that still exist. We are limited, for communications from our world to yours contain truth, contradictions and absurdities, just as religions in your world fail to give mankind a glimpse of the fact that God is infinite mind, striving for the perfection of love. We pray that the tools of science will one day be used to help verify not only the invisible waves of radio, electricity and magnetism, but to understand other etheric frequencies of gravitation, cohesion, life force and even those higher vibrations of the mind world.

At the moment, the swing of life's pendulum seems to be at a turning point. For decades, people have gradually become more dissatisfied with religious teachings and, for comfort, have bathed themselves in the luxuries that scientific technology has provided. By the turn of the century, it will be realised that this materialistic age has not given man the spiritual knowledge that he sub-consciously seeks. The superstitions of all religions will be replaced by a thirst for truth as the garbage is swept to one side. It will be accepted that psychics, mediums and scientists may all play their part in searching for this truth. It is common knowledge that, at present, many pretend to have gifts of the spirits and that this pretence is solely for the purpose of taking advantage of the bereaved, the lonely, the desperate and those who are gullible. The days of these pretenders are coming to an end. The wheat will be separated from the chaff. I am told that all this is part of a great plan devised by those great minds who know the needs of every part of God's creation. It would seem that great mind needs servants who are willing and able to sweep earth clean of those who have thoughts only for self. All the mistakes made by religions of the past and the present will be rectified by those who have been willing to listen - and yet the pendulum of evolution will continue to swing until this particular solar system has served its purpose. When that moment arrives, mind will simply find another section of creation where the tools of matter provide even greater opportunities for progress.

Mankind has now progressed to a stage when he no longer needs thoughts of organised religion to point the way ahead. Amongst the many false teachings within the books of religion lie many truths. If man seeks then, he will find, but spiritual food will never be served to those who are not hungry. Whatever you give to others you will receive back - although I cannot guarantee "a hundredfold". The hidden meaning of this saying does not only apply to the living, but also to those in invisible dimensions. As we share our knowledge with others, those in higher levels of mind share their wisdom with us without counting the cost. Invisible friends gather round every individual waiting for them to listen. Whether in our dimension or yours, those who draw close to us are of similar mind frequency and can only disclose those truths they have found. Sensuous people gather around them sensuous friends. Try, then, to strive for greater things and greater minds will supply that which you need and deserve.

Amongst those who adopt any particular religion, we find vast differences of thought so that, in a sense, there are as many religions as there are individual minds. We in this group urge you to search, to share, to give, to receive, to love and to listen to those who are members of your spiritual family. Just as you have belonged to many earthly families, so you have, and will, belong to many spiritual families as you continue your journey along that pathway of learning. Some of us have turned learning into a joy instead of a pain. We crave the forgiveness of those whom we might have upset in expressing the truth as we understand it. Revive - live again. Remember - bring back part of memory. Reincarnation - incarnate again. Religion - think again.

Evidence for Survival and God

Chapter 12

EVIDENCE FOR SURVIVAL AND GOD

Forgive me if I repeat some of the facts already stated in previous chapters, but every teacher knows that telling once is not enough. Even in physics it is often necessary to refer to lessons already learned before proceeding to greater theories or experiments. It is said that the workman is known by his work. The mind of the composer is reflected in the music that we hear, just as a painting expresses the ideas of the painter. Look around you and see that which is not the work of man. Intelligence would suggest that everything in the heavens, in nature and even in all of science, is the result of an infinite creative mind, of which we are but one infinitesimal part. My son, Raymond, joins me once again, trying to express my thoughts in poetic language:

> Look in God's garden and behold
> The picture that before you will unfold.
> In every flower there is great variation,
> Telling part of the story of creation.
> In science too much truth abides
> About the heavens, the earth and even the tides.
> Pause for a moment, look around you and see
> That infinite mind in every branch and tree.
> Learning is painful but, I'm sure you'll find
> Joy in understanding mysteries of every kind.
> One day you will then realise
> That science and nature are both very wise,
> For together in life they give us the measure
> So that we can find some of God's treasure.
> Our world and your world working together
> Give knowledge that life is truly for ever.
> Bury not then your head in the sand
> Be aware spirit friends hold your hand,
> Guiding you onward, so one day you'll be
> A beautiful butterfly just like me.
> Infinity truly stretches both ways
> For one much wiser than me says.
> Out there and in there, below and above
> Lies God's gift to all - infinite love.

With regard to the formation of worlds, including earth, I can only repeat that, upon physical death, one finds oneself in a level of consciousness with others of like mind. The fact that one is met by old friends who have died, brings a realisation that the physical body has been discarded, yet one still feels the same. I "died" and arrived here; I was not met by any person who had the answers to the mysteries of birth, life and death - I am still searching and am no nearer to understanding these mysteries. My world is a similar world to yours in the fact that what exists in the future is not known with any surety. We are privileged to meet souls wiser than ourselves; they tell of conditions that prevail in their level of mind, but we too can either believe them or turn a deaf ear.....nobody wants to listen - and yet. And yet...what they say gives more sense, reason and purpose to existence than any hypothesis any of us could postulate. Similarly, you who read these words can conclude that the mind of the writer is truly influenced by invisible friends or that the right hemisphere of his physical brain is over-developed in imaginative capabilities. Just as you hope and pray that what the future holds is even brighter than the present conditions, so we hope that those higher spheres are even more harmonious than that in which we now exist.

The theory of natural selectivity without any intelligence to guide it is absurd. It stands as much chance as being possible as hoping that, if all the stones of Westminster Abbey were thrown in the air, they would land in the shape of a beautiful cathedral. We have to strive for an understanding of God, of birth, of life, and of rebirth just as you do, so we cannot give mankind the physical proof that he seeks. Proof of God and of progressing eternally is a personal duty for individuals in both visible and invisible worlds. I often say to earthly friends that I do not like the term "Spirit World", for it suggests that we exist on a planet in some distant solar system. We consist of those sub-atomic particles that are not subject to changes of state - the protons and electrons. The essence of our being consists of finer particles; the type and rate of vibration determines whether we live in astral, etheric, mental or spiritual spheres, all with their subdivisions of levels of consciousness.

As far as God is concerned, we suggest for the moment that whatever exists has a cause. Scientific theories postulate that all solar systems, galaxies and other heavenly bodies came from a big bang. Who caused this big bang and with what purpose? It could be said that natural forces of electricity, gravity, cohesion, temperature and heat were responsible for this initial explosion, but from where did

112

all these natural forces come? Everything that exists has a cause; nothing comes from nothing. We cannot trace the beginning of things for there was no beginning, just as there is no end. Scientists, theologians and philosophers will one day conclude that infinite intelligence was and is responsible for everything that exists, whether visible or invisible, and that God is just as good a word for this infinite force and energy as any other. In the meantime, you and we can only postulate, initiate and meditate on thoughts that substantiate the reality of God. If, as a result of this, we can find no beginning to all things, how dare we suggest an end?

We in invisible dimensions constantly try to find means whereby vibrations can be lowered sufficiently for some to be aware of our presence. Generally only those who can subdue their five physical senses can use their sixth sense to discern us, although sometimes we can even influence matter if there is sufficient psychic physical energy available. This is when physical phenomena occurs and external intelligence directs it. I would like to stress the word external, for phenomena can occur and be governed by minds of incarnate individuals. The only difference between yourselves and ourselves is that we do not have the handicap of the physical. You are mind, we are mind. Either of us can influence matter providing the right conditions prevail. In gathering evidence that suggests the reality of the invisible world, it is good to remember that not all psychic phenomena is due to intervention from the "Spirit World". Allow me to repeat the thought that I expressed when living on earth. Only a vast collection of psychic experiences can contribute towards a definite conclusion that mind is a separate entity from the physical brain. The fact that levitation, materialisation, direct voice, spirit photography, clairvoyance, clairaudience and a host of other phenomena takes place, does not necessarily give evidence of survival. Many earthly minds have proved that they can influence matter. Even when information is given that is outside the knowledge of the recipient, it could be claimed that the medium concerned is using distant telepathy. How then does mankind obtain irrefutable evidence of the survival of human personality?

Scientists have to widen the horizon of their experiments to include forces that do not obey the laws of physics. Some have already done this in proving that matter is no obstacle to many subatomic particles. If only they could put more emphasis on this work, they would discover that intelligence - mind - makes use of some of the higher vibrations of those particles. Instead, they still concentrate on the use of those particles of matter which provide greater earthly comfort.

Most religions still subscribe to rather ancient beliefs instead of trying to replace belief by knowledge. My friend Findlay has fervently traced the origin of most religions and written extensively on these matters, yet few desire the fruits of his labour. However, the fact remains that ideas of survival in many religions owe their origin to the rising and setting of the sun. He lists the many great souls who, in centuries past, have returned to earth to share their spiritual wisdom. The state of your world today shows that, even in history, nobody wanted to listen - and yet great souls even today still return, trying to turn man's eyes away from materialism towards a new age of reason and awareness. I entreat you to become aware of the curse of ignorance by reading some of his research into religious origins. It seems a pity that the natural gift of telepathy has been subdued by both religious superstitions and scientific dogma.

How then can you obtain evidence of immortality if it cannot yet be given by religion or science? Look inside instead of outside. Do your own research, instead of relying on that of others. I realise now that many of the mysteries of creation had their answers deep in the fathoms of my own mind, but when living on earth, they were buried by scientific materialism and religious superstitions. As you discount priestly thoughts within religious books, you will find some true philosophy spoken by those teachers who came to earth with a message - "Seek and you will find. Knock and it will be opened" - but listen to the inner self, for your level of consciousness may be higher than that of those whom you ask. The many books that you read often contain just the opinions of the authors. Even those that claim to have been written by inspiration contain only the thoughts of invisible friends who do not have all the answers. In your investigation of yourself and others, sort out the wheat from the chaff. Only accept that which rings true in the depths of your own mind. This naturally applies to all that you read in this book, for our opening poem stated that we did not have the answers to all of God's mysteries and secrets. Life is an infinite maze in which we often lose the way and have to go back hoping to find the true way. Both science and religion are just useful signposts on our journey, but be careful, for sometimes some interfering soul tries to misguide us by turning the signpost round. Better to use one's own inner guidance instead of relying upon any thoughts contained within both science and religion.

Evidence is a personal matter. Collect it as you journey

onwards and, eventually, its abundance will become so overwhelming that the tools of science and religion will be replaced by your own spiritual vibrations. I now know that it was my son Raymond who influenced the movement of a table in Mariemont. Family and friends often sat with hands on a small table, praying that by this means our minds would be influenced by those who had departed. Sometimes it was excellent, whilst many times it would not make any sense. In the same context, my sittings with Mrs. Piper were evidential yet, on some occasions, her control, Phinuit, seemed to speak nonsense. Now I more clearly understand the difficulties of forming a reliable link between our two worlds. As I, at this moment, influence the medium's mind, I am reminded of a book I enjoyed reading called "Romance of Two Worlds" by Marie Correlli and I take this opportunity of encouraging this medium to read it.

If only science and religion could amalgamate, then it would be understood that God did create the world but, in doing so, it necessitated a reduction of vibrations from pure mind to etheric and then to matter. This process would involve the reverse of a nuclear reaction - a big bang followed by the gradual transformation from radiation into matter. As the various elements assembled, conditions on this planet slowly became suitable for mind to make use of matter for the sole purpose of learning. If the thoughts of religious clergy were removed from all sacred books, then the messages of those great souls and teachers would enmesh with the knowledge of astronomers and men of science. Religion may have been necessary in centuries past, but the group here feel that it has served its purpose. Science, too, should include studies of the energies and vibrations associated with psychometry, telepathy and invisible particles. As this takes place, that which is invisible will become just as real as that which can be perceived by the five physical senses. Evidence of an infinite mind manifests in the whole of nature and science, but up to now, man has only accepted that which has appealed to physical being. A Venus Fly-catching plant displays great ability to sense, even without a physical brain or nervous system. Evidence of invisible forces is as abundant as evidence of that which can be seen, but so far man insists on using the visible to test the invisible. More time should be spent on the investigation of dreams, telepathy, precognition and the multitude of strange phenomena that do not obey scientific laws. We suggest that, if this took place, man would discover that there are parallel universes that correspond to the development of mind.

115

Apart from influencing earthly mind I have, since my death, had the opportunity of speaking through an ectoplasmic voice box. My son, Raymond, has materialised - and yet, because of the limitations of physical phenomena, very few people were aware of our communications. If the available energy is used for the forming of physical matter, then there is less energy available for the purpose of communication. It is because of this that we take the opportunity of expressing our thoughts through this channel. I have no doubt that this medium will suffer abuse, just as my friend Crookes suffered. It would seem that those who are willing to help provide much-needed evidence are all persecuted in one way or another. Even when I was in America giving a scientific lecture, the chairman introduced me as a person who believed he could contact the dead. My friend Conan Doyle was introduced as a man who believed in fairies. Galileo was imprisoned because he discovered a truth - the earth is a sphere and revolves around the sun. We therefore apologise for any ideas that may have offended any reader - yet the truth often hurts.

It is hard for the butterfly to communicate with the world that it left - the caterpillar world - yet deep within the simple minds of all caterpillars lies an expectation of a better world. Gather evidence from those who have a true spiritual gift, but also dig deep into the depths of your own soul. There you will find knowledge and experience that you have gathered in many experiences. You will also find intuitive feelings, vibrations that whisper in your etheric ear, telling you of a finer world than the prison in which you now exist.

Life

Chapter 13

LIFE

Once again, I must apologise if I repeat any ideas already mentioned in previous chapters, but we are servants to the constant enquiry of this medium between two worlds. The thoughts that reach us at this moment desire a better understanding of the difference between that which is lifeless and that which is living. Somewhere in the midst of these thoughts we hear a voice that would seem to say "Does each cell of my body have a soul? Do all the germs and viruses that often invade my body have a spirit? Are they individuals in their own right? Does the sperm within my being live like microscopic insects? The cry that we hear can only be stemmed by an understanding of life.

It is common knowledge that seeds found in pyramids have been planted and germinate. It could be asked whether life lay dormant in these seeds or whether life only started when the seeds were planted. Is the ovarian egg alive before being fertilised by sperm or does life start only at conception? With regard to all these problems, we as a group can only repeat the thoughts that have been given to us by those in higher levels of mind than ourselves. Within the ether lie not only the lower vibrations of magnetism, electricity, light, cohesion and gravity, but much higher vibrations including one that can only be defined as "life force". Whether seed, plant, animal or human - all require certain conditions for life to manifest. On this planet, these include sunlight, nutritional products supplied by earth's elements, as well as a union with the invisible life force. The life force is rather like an animated magnetism. It is a force field containing the elemental and vital parts of mind; another name for this could well be the directing principle. When the elements of matter combine to form an organism capable of sustaining life, there is a natural attraction to a level of life force. The motor cannot show locomotion without the invisible electric field. Matter cannot exhibit life without the invisible life force. This force is the link between that which is termed spirit and matter. It is, as I suggested before, the lower levels of mind - those that are necessary to sustain life. The higher levels of mind are those levels that include reasoning, intellect, self-awareness, love and individuality.

Mankind tends to feel that in the "Spirit World" there are many spheres with their sub-divisional levels of consciousness. This is true, but below the "Spirit World" lie other levels that may not be termed spirit but only life force. It is often said that nature abhors a vacuum. If the vessel encasing a vacuum is broken, then air is drawn in, filling the space. In those lower kingdoms, where spirit is not yet manifest, life force is drawn into the vehicle at the moment of fertilisation. It is well known that a worm may be bisected, resulting in two lives instead of one. A stone may be broken into many pieces. In the case of the stone, only the etheric energies of cohesion have been sub-divided; in the case of the worm, higher etheric vibrations - those of life force - have been divided. These forces include self-preservation, self-healing, propagation of species and other energies embraced by the elemental and vital elements of mind. Although certain plants produce infants in the form of seeds, cuttings may also be taken to produce separate plants. Once again, only mind in its lowest form - life force - may be divided.

We see that in higher kingdoms, such as the animal, this life force has added to itself more delicate layers of mind that include maternal, paternal and even emotional vibrations. It would be correct to refer to the life force of a plant, but not to that of an animal. Mind would be a more appropriate word in the animal kingdom. It would appear that the term spirit could only be used in reference to man who has expanded mind so that it now includes all the layers of life force as well as greater reason, intellect, emotion and higher appreciation of beauty, empathy, sympathy and love. We are told that man's mind is clothed with sufficient etherical and spiritual bodies that it is capable of containing itself as an individual and thus the term "spirit" is used to describe the mind of man. And yet - individuality is only in its infancy on planet earth.

In the invisible spheres attached to earth, spirit continues to progress; mind continues to evolve, adding to itself greater understanding of God's creation. That is why we, in previous chapters, have referred to earth as one of an infinite number of nursery schools. Life is eternal, but those in the lower classes can hardly be expected to understand the minds of those who have entered universities. For the moment then, let us concentrate on life in earth's nursery school, praying that greater understanding of it may gain us entrance into those higher grades.

As we look around the nursery school, we see that some students live in under-developed countries where poverty, malnutrition, pain and suffering prevail. Others seem to dwell in places surrounded by luxuries, wealth, fine houses and even servants. It would seem

120

that, if we only have one physical life with no hereafter, then life is grossly unfair. Can there be any sensible answer to this state of affairs? The nature part of God may supply some answers, for your pet peacock, dog or cat may also feel under-privileged when they observe you and your life. The mind of the animal friend has a vehicle suitable for it. Even in other kingdoms we can observe conditions of hardship and also those of a more comfortable and easy nature. Maybe even the sandstone wishes it were a diamond. Conditions of extreme variety exist in all kingdoms. The diamond was not always a diamond. It only achieved this state by other minerals becoming subject to extreme pressure and temperature.

The fact that man's mind has gained individuality does not afford him peace, joy, good health and all the conditions of a Utopian world. All the range of conditions that exist in the many countries give mind and spirit a wealth of learning opportunity. I can remember that war conditions encouraged a greater spirit of comradeship than that which exists in an affluent society. Conditions of poverty help the mind to gain appreciation of a crust of bread. Often in affluent parts of the world jealousy, greed and selfishness abound. That infinite mind saw that even individualised mind - spirit - needs a range of extreme conditions so that, in many experiences, it may rise above all that is material or physical. How can any soul appreciate wealth unless it has experienced poverty? How can any soul understand grief unless he has experienced it? The variety of conditions that exist on earth provide the spirit with limited opportunities of acquiring knowledge and experience. These two qualities give the soul wisdom. Only the wise man is aware of God's omniscience. The purpose of life is living, for living gives learning, learning gives experience, experience gives wisdom and wisdom gives greater awareness of the infinite mind.

The term life not only applies to those who are incarnate, but also to us in the real world. Those in higher levels or spheres of consciousness are more alive than those in the lower. Life on earth gives the spirit an awareness of the vast difference in levels of man's mind. Here we live amongst like minds and now, armed with earthly experiences, have a knowledge giving us the desire to live better, to learn more and to love better. One much wiser than myself would encourage us all constantly to be thankful that we are what we are.

The cells of your body have life force and, when they die, that life force is drawn back to its appropriate level. Others take their place and they are pleased to be servants to a greater force - your

121

spirit. Your spirit, although an individual, is part of a level of consciousness. Be pleased to be a part of that level, for that level in itself is part of a greater whole - ad infinitum. The conductor of this universal orchestra is, of course, that infinite mind, beyond both your and our conception - God. The parts of the body are rather like the physical musical instruments, with your mind as the musician. As you play your instrument, have regard for other members of the orchestra, but in particular the leaders of various sections. Most of all, keep one eye on the conductor, for without him there would be disharmony and possibly chaos. Nobody wants to listen - and yet the conductor waits to lead his orchestra in creating the finest celestial and divine music. Within creation there is not only the earthly orchestra, but an infinite number who learn to combine together, making the sound of creation even finer and finer.

Our thoughts on life have so far been confined to the waking part of life. Living does not only imply playing and working, through which we learn. Life on earth also involves states of semiconsciousness, unconsciousness and dreams. These altered levels of consciousness play a great part in the development of the soul. Dreaming is the state in which we are able to recall experiences of all the past, the present and even, sometimes, a glimpse of the future. It is a state in which we can review all levels through which we have evolved, as well as receiving guidance for those experiences yet to come. In this state, we are able to be with the many friends we have met in all previous experiences, as well as meeting other living souls who are also in a state of sleep. It could be said that you die daily for, during nightly sleep, the spirit is released from its earthly prison to enter the real world - the world of the mind. Once free of the body, it can use its creative abilities without the handicaps of time, distance and speed.

We have already stated that the conditions of each level are made by the creative ability of the minds of its inhabitants. Sleep, therefore, gives the spirit a necessary freedom to exercise its creative thoughts and ideas. In a sense it is completely freed from its physical shell. Do not be surprised if your dream world is strange to you. Released from earthly inhibitions you find yourself in the state that you will enter after death. This release enables some who are instantly freed from matter to enter the society of others similar, or even superior, to themselves. Others who have been chained by earthly inhibitions, find themselves in levels even lower and baser than those to which they are addicted when conscious. Intelligent sleep is a sign that a person is free of earthly gross and material pursuits. If I could whisper a message in your ear with regard to dreams, it would be "dream well". Those who have great affection for earthly pleasures often find themselves in a state of confusion, for they are in between your unreal world and our real world. Many who are incarnate claim that they cannot remember their dreams. That great architect of creation realised that, if they could, they would never want to return to the prison of earthly flesh. The dream part of life offers the spirit a view of the progress made. I would advise you not to listen to the fortune tellers, who would profess ability in interpreting your dreams, for everybody's dream world is different. The reason for this difference is that, as your spirit enters its deserved level, it takes with it its own past and present experiences, adding to them the advice and wisdom of those whom you meet.

Life, then, gives the soul an opportunity of learning during waking hours, then returning home to see if that learning has earned the spirit greater freedom, greater beauty, greater light and understanding of the true meaning and purpose of eternal life. The master mind that has planned all, has decreed that those on earth cannot appreciate all that life offers. Those in earth conditions wish for happiness and immortality. This can be achieved by sowing the seeds of noble thoughts, by good deeds, by helping others to replace hope and faith by knowledge. Life gives you the opportunity to help yourself by helping others to rid themselves of the superstitions, fears, creeds and dogmas that mighty religious organisations have used. Share with others the facts and knowledge that you gain, so that one day mankind will accept life on earth as a challenge. The earthly journey is full of problems, stumbling blocks and obstacles. As these are overcome, the spirit grows richer, preparing for itself conditions that it deserves. Some live a short life whilst others, like myself, travelled that journey for nearly nine decades. As you journey onwards, always have in mind the fact that no matter how long your earthly journey lasts, it is nothing compared with eternity. If the road seems unsure, put your hand in the hands of those who guide you. That is much safer than relying on others around you who are, in truth, just as lost and mystified in life as yourself.

Birth, life and death remind me of a new motor car. When new, the driver cannot show his full skill in driving. He must wait until all the various parts have reached their maximum efficiency - when it is in its prime. After this, the vehicle gradually loses its efficiency as the various parts become worn and often have to be replaced. It is the same driver throughout the total life of the motor car. Similarly in life, the spirit can only express itself fully when its vehicle, the body, is in its prime. Have empathy for both the very young and old, for in these stages of life the spirit often struggles to drive a vehicle that is not lifeworthy.

Is this all life was meant to be
Working, playing and having tea?
Or is there some hidden and greater plan
Involving flowers, animals, woman and man?
Everyone behind a mask does hide,
Full of superstition, selfishness and pride.
Earth is but a speck of dust -
Seek the truth and in God trust.
To the purpose of life be not blind
The invisible world is here to find.
Fear and ignorance of the past
Still seems in man to last.
Those who now have joined us here
Know that death was nothing to fear.
Earthly life is God's nursery school
Your body serves simply as a tool
To learn all secrets and mysteries of life
By overcoming problems, troubles and strife.
So that as life's lessons you slowly learn
A beautiful level of mind you earn.
Only by being of service to others
You will know they are sisters and brothers
In one universal family tree,
Travelling together for eternity.

Abortion, Miscarriage,
Children and Old Age

Chapter 14

ABORTION, MISCARRIAGE, CHILDREN AND OLD AGE

In earlier chapters we have tried to paint a picture of conditions that prevail in our level; that is the level of mind in which our group find ourselves. Apart from the existence of etheric minerals, soil, plants, rivers, seas, animals, birds and other earthly parallel conditions of both scientific and artistic nature, there are children of all ages. Many women have undergone abortion, suffered miscarriages and lost babies. Accidents occur when children of only a few years old make the journey from your world to whatever level of consciousness their soul deserves. Remember, that soul has not only manifested in the life they have just left, but has been evolving in eternity and like adults, even children gravitate to whatever level befits their spiritual specific gravity.

We would like to give some comfort to those parents who have suffered the loss of a child who only spent a short time in earthly conditions. First, let me remind you that the child in question does not suffer in any way but, on the contrary, returns to its real home. The lesson to be learnt is more often for those relatives and friends that are left behind on that limited cabbage leaf of earthly life. The nursery school of earth has its extremes. There is beauty and ugliness, health and illness, strength and weakness and many other opposites, including death at both infancy and old age. As we have already mentioned, these extremes are necessary to enable the students of life to realise that positive and negative conditions also exist in our world. "In our Father's house are many mansions", ranging from those very low, hellish conditions to those celestial levels of spirit that, for the moment, lie beyond our spiritual vision. Without digressing too much, I hope you can appreciate that death must also be included amongst the extremities of conditions that exist in the school of earth, and many wish to know what happens to the souls of those who lose their earthly body at a very young age. The explanation needs great clarification, for many factors must be taken into consideration.

In the astral and etheric levels of mind there are myriads of souls, both male and female, who have never satisfied their paternal or maternal experiences. There are, therefore, quite sufficient "spirit fathers and mothers" always waiting to take care of those who come to our world in the etheric form of infants. Let us say that we have an endless supply of foster parents. Relatives of those infants are also there to meet them, but are engaged in other activities necessary for their own advancement. It is not always possible for a relative to care for their family who arrive in etheric baby clothes. In any case, the spiritual foster parents belong to the same spiritual family of their charge, even though not of the same earthly blood family. These foster parents exist in all levels of consciousness, except of course in those very high spheres where lessons of parenthood were learnt long ago. You will notice that I have referred not only to women who have not had sufficient experience as a mother, but also to men who lack the experience of fatherhood. The fact that I had six sons then six daughters did not guarantee sufficient understanding of being a father. The life as Oliver Lodge only added to experiences I had gained in other lives.

In earthly life, the mind and spirit has to wait for the physical body to grow before that soul may express itself to the full - usually in that part of life that is called prime. Old age often involves a frustration in the fact that the physical body, particularly the brain, ceases to be efficient enough for the spirit to express its experience, knowledge and wisdom. Here conditions are different, for the etheric infant does not have to wait earthly years to reach its prime. Every etheric child that arrives in our dimensions goes to that level that befits its mental and spiritual evolvement; the lower the level of consciousness, the longer it takes for that etheric body to reach maturity. Those highly evolved souls can cast off the etheric garment almost immediately and, therefore, need no etheric foster parents. If a soul needs further experience of childhood and youth, then that experience is provided by those who need experience of fatherhood and motherhood. Naturally, these conditions differ from one level to another. Do not be surprised if communication on these matters varies, for those who communicate with you may only tell of those conditions that prevail in their own and, maybe, lower levels.

For those parents who have been involved in miscarriage, abortion or have lost a child at a very early age, take comfort in the fact that the soul of their baby continues to take an interest in its parents, whether or not it belongs to the same spiritual family. There are cases where the same soul tries more than once to be born into the same earthly family, if not to the same parents then to others in the same earthly family. As we have stated, the time taken for development to maturity varies from level to level, whereas on earth that time is governed by the development of the physical body.

Many must wonder what happens to those relatives or friends who live to a great age, sometimes seeming to suffer from senile dementia and a lack of ability to express themselves. Allow me to repeat from personal experience that it is only the physical brain that cannot replace cells quickly enough to maintain the same efficiency as it did in its prime. The mind and spirit suffer a similar frustration as in the conditions of physical birth. Once that etheric umbilical cord is severed, the etheric brain feels the release and can operate at its maximum once again. This realisation of freedom does, of course, once again, vary from level to level, recovery being faster in higher levels of consciousness. Just as an infant may "grow up" very quickly in those higher levels, so an aged person may "grow younger" very quickly. The time taken for this to occur depends upon the evolvement of the mind and spirit that controls the etheric body. In earthly time, it took me a matter of days to change my etheric old age to that which I considered my prime condition. For communication purposes, I can alter my etheric looks and voice to suit the situation. Those in our group do not even need to retain any etheric garment, except when we wish to help those in lower etheric levels or when we use earthly mediums to communicate our thoughts, voices and mannerisms. In simple words, those who still wear etheric garments can mould them to whatever age they wish. The mind determines the age, looks and even the clothes with which we dress our etheric form. We are as we want to be.

In our world there are children, there are youths and there are old people but the time spent in etheric chapters of life differs greatly to the time spent in earthly conditions. We realise that, whilst on earth, we all tend to speak of our sons or daughters, our mothers and fathers, my aunt Anne, etc., as if those relations belonged to us. Again, I wish to emphasise that although our parents provided us with an earthly vehicle and life force, the spirit and mind are independent of any earthly relatives. The spirit and mind belong to a spiritual family that may sometimes include earthly relatives. This surely explains why, so often, friends seem to be on a closer mental vibration than family. It also explains why some of our sons or daughters seem to be on a different wavelength than ourselves. In joining our earthly family, those souls knew that the environment that we, as parents, could provide was necessary for their spiritual progression. If you feel great spiritual closeness to any of your earthly family, then it is because they belong to the same level of consciousness as yourself - not because they have the same blood running through their veins as runs in your body.

Remember that birth and death are necessary experiences for every soul and, for those who observe these natural phenomena of life, those who spend only a very short time on earth are more fortunate than those who live many years. Earth is the prison of the soul - our world is a world of freedom - the butterfly world.

Origin and Destiny

Chapter 15

ORIGIN AND DESTINY

A thought force came to the first combination of certain elements and acids, giving the product that is called life force - no doubt in some very simple form such as a virus. Other thoughts were received by this first life form enabling it to develop gradually through all the manifestations of life that we witness today. As that life force evolved, it obviously improved the vehicles to which it was attached, until its complexity demanded the even finer vibrations that we call mind, as witnessed in the animal kingdom. Mind and its vehicle became more complex until the day arrived when evolution reached the stage of what could be called sub-man. Only at this stage could one of sub-man form contemplate on "from whence did I come and wither do I go?" That first man would no doubt share his thoughts with his mate. Maybe we should call them Adam and Eve? As those thoughts spread amongst others, mind advanced, wanting to understand the origin of the planet, the life upon it and also death. These thoughts gave birth to both science, in its many forms, and religion.

We have made some progress in both of these studies, for anatomy, biology and medical sciences have given us some glimpses of the wonders of earthly vehicles whether in insect, fish, plant, animal or human form. The observance of the great forces of the sun, moon, thunder and lightning, fire and others caused man to presume that these forces were under the control of higher intelligences than himself. Thus it was that Gods were visualised and idols made to represent them. Religion was born.

Astronomy has proved to man that his planet earth is but a speck of dust compared with that which he has seen through his modern mechanical and electrical telescopes. It is now accepted that this solar system is but one of trillions in a single galaxy called "the Milky Way" and that the Milky Way is only one of trillions within the observance of astronomers. By careful investigation, it has been proved that galaxies are the result of immense whirling masses of gas, called spiral nebulae, and the origin of these lies in a theory of a great explosion called "the big bang". This may be so, but who caused this big bang and from where did he get all the stuff to create it? Science is still searching for answers.

Religion has also made some progress; just a little - for now

133

man accepts that the forces belonging to the sun, moon, lightning, fire, etc., are just part of what is called nature. The religious thoughts of ancient philosophers suggested that some great God over all other Gods created this planet in six days, then rested on the seventh. In those days it was thought that the earth was the centre of creation and that all other forms of life were subservient to man. Religion and science have been in conflict since those days of sub-man. Great scientists such as Galileo, Copernicus, Bruno and others have been tortured, persecuted and executed for suggesting that the ecclesiastics of the time were wrong. Even today, science is used to ridicule religion, as religion uses scientific inventions to torture, maim, kill and wage war. Is it possible that they are both correct? Maybe those ancient philosophers used days instead of gigantic periods of time. After all, six days plus one other adds up to seven, the same number as colours in the rainbow, white keys on the piano from C to B, wonders of the world, days of the week, energy centres of the body, seas of the earth, as well as other phenomena. Maybe they expressed their thoughts as to origin in metaphorical language; maybe all the scientific facts concerning the origin of creation can be divided into seven stages of evolution. Certainly there are forces of gravitation, cohesion, magnetism, electricity and life that scientists have not yet fully explained. Without doubt, many of the thoughts expressed in the bible are not the thoughts of one of life's great teachers, but are the thoughts of greedy, selfish, power-seeking religious clerics of old. Scientists cannot prove that the theory of one big bang is correct. If infinite space is a reality then maybe big bangs have been taking place throughout eternity. Only when sensible men in both science and religion join their thoughts and knowledge will any real progress be made.

In considering the origin of all things, we must realise that matter enables us to use our five physical senses and also acts as something through which we become aware of invisible forces. We would never become aware of light, electricity, magnetism or other invisible forms of energy unless they affected matter. There are other forms of energy that are higher than those that exist within etheric wavelengths, for all the forces bound by the substance ether are limited in their speed. The mind world simply uses etheric vibrations so that they, in turn, affect the physical world. The mind world therefore utilises vibrations within a region capable of exceeding the limitations of ether. In higher regions still are what may be termed vibrations of spirit that use mind to influence etheric and, thus, the physi-

134

cal world. When spirit vibrations put the importance of individuality to one side, vibrations of a celestial form exist. Above those lie that pure, infinite intelligence that, for want of a better name we call God. The existence of all these spheres are due to just a thought from that infinite intelligence. There lies the origin of creation - we and everything around us are just the result of that thought. Other thoughts from that infinite intelligence provide an eternal adventure for us, being part of it. Certain parts of both science and religion are correct, providing we use intellect in interpreting the theories and philosophies that are common. Through matter, we become aware of parts of the universe, but we must allow for invisible forces that do not conform to the laws of physical science.

I would now substitute the biblical words "In the beginning was the word" for "in our beginning was a thought", and that thought was responsible for everything in both visible and invisible worlds. That thought was only one from that infinite intelligence; it gave that intelligence an opportunity of infinite expansion by allowing simple law and order to progress through life force, etheric, mind, spirit and celestial vibrations so that, finally, it could add to that which we call God - infinite intelligence. Other thoughts from the same source have no doubt been responsible for similar expansion in other regions of creation. Some recent phenomena suggests that intelligences greater than that of mankind exist in those other regions and that they are trying to make us aware of their reality. We, in our level of consciousness, do not have sufficient proof of these intelligences, but at least we can confirm that mind and spirit do not need a physical body.

As for your and our destiny, I have already suggested that God is forever thinking of new adventures. Our destiny is to become part of that great intelligence that has always existed. We are children of father science and mother nature, whose laws have always been there. In our evolution, we simply learn to understand those laws, eventually becoming aware that most of them are beyond the physical and material world. How can either those incarnate or discarnate souls give answers to what lies ahead on an eternal journey? Is it not sufficient for now for those who dwell in your world or in ours to be able to say "I am"?

In many of my books I contended that ether was the only means whereby spirit could act upon matter. This fact I still support, but see now that spirit uses mind to effect the etheric. Celestial intelligences have an influence on individual spirits and that infinite intel-

135

ligence. God uses all these lower vibrations so that his thoughts may become manifest. We apologise to those who read these thoughts, but ask that you understand the limitations of our communication, which depends upon the mind tools of the medium we are privileged to use. That is the reason why we may seem to be different when we use other available receivers of our thoughts. Most of the chapters of my life are contained in voluminous books written by myself and others, so that it is difficult to give you information that is not already common knowledge. If I were to admit that I succumbed to temptation by a lady of the streets of London as I made my way home from the lectures of Tydall, it would not serve as proof of my identity. Read what is written and, if the contents appeal to your sense of reason and intellect, then keep an open mind as to the origin of the thoughts expressed.

We as a group cannot share any more thoughts with you on origin or destiny, for to do so would only repeat astronomical facts and show that most religions are still ignorant of the origin and destiny of mankind. If there is a great resurrection, then it has already taken place, for we are here. If life, in some form, found its origin in some other region of space, we can neither confirm or deny it. We can sometimes use etheric vibrations to affect material objects, but then so can you. There is one in your midst to-day who can perform miracles, produce apports and heal the sick yet, in proportion to the world's population, "nobody wants to listen - and yet - I am".

Yesterday and Today

Chapter 16

YESTERDAY AND TODAY

As a scientist, I feel that the history of science can boast of many achievements, yet there is no doubt that it has also been an obstruction, for theories that seem proven are loath to make room for new truths. History is full of examples in which anatomists, astronomers and scientists were persecuted for daring to disagree with well-established theories. If the discoveries of Galileo were ridiculed by both science and religion, it is no wonder that the investigations by both myself and William Crookes were looked at askance and disbelieved. The publishing of Darwin's theory comes almost within my living memory, for both my paternal grandfathers were members of the clergy and ecclesiastics of that time were most upset by the suggestion - nay - proof, that life as they knew it came about by gradual evolution.

In this ethereal group, even Franz was forced to leave Paris when King Louis XVI sympathised with the medical men, who ridiculed his theory of a magnetic fluid. Phillippe, also, was criticised for continuing studies of what, today, is the accepted phenomenon of hypnosis. A book called "Sir O.L. & Spiritualism" was written by a person who felt that men of science should not involve themselves in the study of mediumship. It was during my lifetime that even the discovery of antiseptics received great opposition from ecclesiastics. They seemed to think that pain was one of the prime punishments of the devil - whoever he is. No doubt I will be criticised again as I refer to the superstitions that prevailed and still prevail in the majority of religions. Mankind, generally, still clings to ancient belief instead of replacing it by knowledge. The level of mind called intellect shouts the fact that no singular religion is correct - not even spiritualism. History reveals the fact that it was thought that the spirit resided in the bowels, blood, liver or other organs of the physical body. Those who did not accept these superstitions were tortured, persecuted and put to death. The group assembled here have no physical bodies, yet each one of us can say "I am". Anatomy and medical science have advanced, but not enough, for today many feel that the brain and mind are one and the same. The protoplasmic organs and cells of the body are instruments of the brain, enabling great locomotion, but the brain is simply an instrument enabling the mind to express itself in physical actions.

In the above, I stated my opinion that not even spiritualism contained all truth. Even though it asserts that communication with the dead is possible, it fails to admit that communication is often limited to discussion with those in the etheric world who do not know a great deal more than when they were alive. Just as orthodox religion is sub-divided, so spiritualism suffers from a similar division. There are those who believe that the Nazarene was the true representative of that infinite intelligence - God - whilst others seem afraid even to mention the name Jesus, preferring to direct their prayers to something they do not even try to comprehend. Whilst discussing spiritualism, we in our group feel that it has fallen into a state of decay, similar to that seen in other religions. I can remember taking many of my friends to see Mrs. Piper. Most times, as a precautionary measure they were introduced to the medium by pseudonyms, yet Mrs. Piper gave correct names of both my earthly friends and their relatives dwelling in invisible dimensions. Similar credit could be given to many other mediums of that time. The Witchcraft Act of 1735 was still in force and education had only just become compulsory. There was no wireless as there is today. The phenomenon of the Fox sisters was making rapid progress and many took an interest in table tilting. There was hope that we would not have to lie in our graves until the great resurrection replaced the fear that many religions taught at that time. An evening spent with friends involved singing around the piano, table turning or discussing both life and death.

It would seem that the great advances in science, anatomy, education, printing and freedom of speech, have helped to rid mankind of some religious superstition. An understanding of the origin of the earth has replaced the story of creation: people are more free to be atheist or follow a religion of their choice. Most put intellect to one side and, as in political matters, follow the same thoughts as their parents. All this greater knowledge and freedom seem to have made mankind more physical and materialistic. Science is only just beginning to extend its horizon to include forces, energies and vibrations that lie well outside the laws of earthly physics. Scientists of today seem afraid to admit that levitation and other phenomena contradict the laws of gravity and speed of light. Mediums of today still address a personified God in their prayers. Supplications for peace, animal welfare, the sick and for other plagues of mankind, are made, hoping that God or spirit guides will save mankind from having to put right all that is wrong. In general, the invisible world can only impinge thoughts on the minds of those willing to listen.

Nobody wants to listen - and yet we, in that invisible world, have eternity to continue trying to make man realise that:

Now he needs not wonder why
All that lives has to die,
For when we left our bodies behind,
A new and better life we all did find.
Although man may venture into different lands,
His destiny lies within his own hands.

If spiritualism is ever to become a universal philosophy, it will have to shift its emphasis on personal communication to embrace other spiritual gifts. Not every sensitive capable of discerning spirit has the gift of knowledge and wisdom. Would it not be better to listen to the experience of some person who has clinically died than sing "Abide with me"? Some doctor or nurse could be invited to speak on the death-bed visions they have witnessed. The gift of healing could also be demonstrated as part of any meeting. If music is to play a part in any gathering, let it be of a quality that raises the vibrations. Galileo had the courage to show that the earth is not the centre of creation. Who has the courage to say that spiritualist meetings of today are not the epitome of perfection? They seem to suffer from the same ritual disease as the more orthodox religions. Jealousy, self-aggrandisement and personal gain seem to be other diseases that have made the spiritualism of today quite sick. There is no doubt that not all spiritualists are spiritual. We take this opportunity of urging you to become seekers of truth, rather than sheep that follow a shepherd who does not know the way. How can we give "cross-correspondence" today when mediums are jealous of one another's gifts? The mediums of old such as Piper, Leonard, Willet, Sloan and others have been replaced mainly by sensitives who obtain most of their information from the auric fields of those to whom they speak. Spiritualists must be educated to differentiate between psychic sensitivity and true mediumship.

Dying does not give one an immediate understanding of all things material, ethereal, mental or spiritual. It is more akin to the process of birth, when, no doubt, we all wondered where we had arrived and sensed the proximity of friends, some of whom seemed closer than others. I'm sure the new-born feels the world both strange and familiar. This second birth gives a temporary forgetfulness of from whence we have come, but with help we remember the experiences, mistakes and good deeds that we have just left behind. Some memories we are pleased to forget, yet benefit is obtained from all the experiences gained in the incidents of life. I am pleased to remember that I and my sons Alex and Brodie were instrumental in the invention of the spark plug, dust collection by heat (then electricity) and other useful tools for society. All of my scientific work did not make me any wiser or more spiritual than the ordinary man. Now I am more sure than ever that many ordinary people of my time were much more charitable than myself.

It is true that I suggested there were more particles within the atom than those of which scientists of my day were aware. In all these matters I have not made any great progress since 22nd August 1940 - the day of my rebirth - except for the fact that I now confirm that there are particles much finer than those within the limitations of etheric wavelengths. The thoughts expressed in these chapters are, therefore, only opinions in the light of experiences in both caterpillar and butterfly worlds. Experience gained in earthly life equipped me for a better understanding of the level in which I and my friends dwell. We have, with help, reviewed the earthly life we left and become aware of not only personal mistakes but also the failings of science, religion and politics in helping mankind to sort out the wheat from the chaff. Our comments about science, religion and politics are made in an effort to help people realise the truth. It appears that infinity not only exists in outer space, but also within the atom itself. Some in your world are kind enough to suggest that I and fellow scientists were pioneers in the discovery of these matters. We only postulated theories that suggested there was more to the atom "than met the eye".

I am pleased to see that, today, one or two men of science are at last becoming convinced of the necessity and reality of the forces which use the ether as a medium. They even accept the fact that there are parallel universes to earthly and physical vibrations. Neither scientific instruments nor abstract mathematics will ever help them to measure or become convinced of those vibrations that lie beyond etheric frequencies. Physical instruments exist that can measure the forces of electricity, magnetism, gravity and even the minute electromagnetic impulses of a physical brain, but it must be accepted that only mental instruments can detect the transmissions of the mind and spirit. This will involve close co-operation between scientists and mediums. When both science and mediums become less materialistically-minded, they may turn their eyes towards helping those who are grief-stricken and brain-washed by religious superstition and even realise the truths and laws that prevail in invisible worlds. Your world is full of tension, stress, worry and grief, mainly based on physical and material matters. What is one lifetime compared with eternity?

I have referred to the wonderful gifts of some of the mediums of my day whose work was judged by the continued evidence they were able to give to those who sought proof of the survival of their loved ones. Their work spoke for itself, in a similar manner to the music of the great composers. I understand that, today, in spiritualism, there are those who wish to put themselves in a position to judge developing mediums. Who judged Mrs. Piper? Who is going to examine the credentials of the examiners? One may be able to test knowledge of the bible with those who aspire to become members of the clergy, but testing the inspiration of sensitives is surely a very different matter. At the same time, I do realise that, in your day, there are public demonstrations of mediumship, where it is important that only those with experience should be invited to demonstrate. I remember days when the mediumship of Mrs. Piper and Mrs. Leonard would not have pleased any examiner. We implore those in authority to encourage those who are trying to improve the quality of their awareness. Surely this would be better achieved by providing education in these matters rather than just an examination. Even great musicians and artists are not always in excellent form. Do not allow political religion to discourage those who are willing to try, otherwise it may be a modern "burning of witches". A relative of this medium does not even claim to be inspired, yet we feel his words may give comfort to many who mourn. It would be a pity if these words should never be heard and it is my privilege, with his permission, to quote them:

> Shed your tears a hundred-fold
> From the thorns you have to bear,
> But drink not from the cup of bitterness
> Of pity and despair.
> The light you held so dearly
> Was fashioned like a gem,
> With scintillating facets
> To shine from each of them.
> It seems this gem He loaned to you
> So precious and so rare,

He needed rather urgently
To light a mansion there.
When grief has turned to memories
With time to heal the pain,
Divide those broken pieces of your heart
Into loving light again.
Give that light to darkened places
Comfort and joy to saddened faces.
And at the final calling
When all the brightness is one
You'll shine with all your loved ones
Much brighter than the sun.

Thinking of yesterday and today, I remember being with Myers on Richet's island - witnessing the phenomena of Eusapia Palladino. We sometimes spoke in French - "J'ai le main droit", "J'ai le main gauche". For those not familiar with this language, one of us held the right hand of the medium whilst another held the left hand. Although objects moved and sometimes materialised forms could be seen, this did not prove intervention from external minds. In fact, I now know that, when the energy ebbed, the medium took advantage of the few times when we did not hold her hands. Even her invisible spirit friends would sometimes realise that, in order to accomplish a certain action, they had to move the physical limbs of the medium. I understand from my friends Myers and Crookes that, in the phenomenon of materialisation, it was not always possible to materialise a solid figure. Ectoplasm was sometimes draped over the physical body of the medium. If any person had shone a bright light, no doubt those present would have cried fraud when they saw only the physical body of the medium. Houdini demonstrated the fact that the investigators can resort to stupid actions when they realise they cannot explain the phenomenon that they witness. I realise that many times my conclusions in these matters were wrong. Great physical mediums of the past often stooped to acts that deceived those in attendance. Now I realise that this was done to please those present, since they demanded "the show must go on". We in our group ask you not to be hasty in your judgment. Only a continued investigation over a period of time gives one the right to reach a conclusion as to the validity of an experiment, whether it be scientific or mediumistic.

After my son Raymond died, he managed to communicate the fact that, in his level of consciousness, he could partake of a whisky and soda. Many spiritualists at that time felt that this communication was untrue and that the "spirit world" did not need the delights of earthly pleasures. In low levels of mind there are more brothels, drinking houses and other similar pursuits than ever existed in earthly conditions. The invisible world has its desire levels in each level of consciousness. What is hell to one may be heaven to another - each to his own.

In the past the scientific community attacked me for being religious and the theological men were critical of my scientific outlook. In life, it was my desire to blend both science and religion. That task still prevails and now I realise more than ever that this undertaking is on-going. In fact, it would seem that pendulums swing in all walks of life - in fashion, music, art and all things that arouse the interest and enthusiasm of mankind. It is because of this desire to join the truths in both science and religion that we here work as a group. We realise that, if and when these writings are given to the public, our brother Raymond will no doubt be subjected to even greater ridicule than he has already suffered. As we continue to transmit thoughts, we pray that he has the strength to stand by the truth in the same manner as did Galileo, Jean d'Arc and others of the past.

My friend Findlay has written extensively on the origin of most religions. He has shown how man, in his ignorance, would first make Gods of the sun, moon and forces of nature. It would serve no purpose for me to repeat that which has already been written. We only wish to verify that much that is written in the bible, and even other religious books, is the philosophy of the ecclesiastics of days long ago. Even men of science used to think that the atom was the building block of all matter. Now it is realised that an atom is just one form in which energy manifests. Many of Newton's laws were put to one side as Einstein's theories gripped the thoughts of the scientific world. Religions suggested that life resulted in either promotion to heavenly realms or demotion into regions of hell. They were all wrong.

Both Newton and Einstein imparted great understanding of the forces of which they were aware, but both took into consideration only the forces that appertain to matter and the lower vibrations of the etheric semi-physical world. We now have a greater understanding of forces that can affect these two regions. In a previous chapter I tried to show how there is an interaction between the vibrations of the physical, etheric, mind and spirit worlds. Neither of these two great men took into consideration how high intelligences in the invisible world can influence the lower, more physical, vibrations of both matter and etheric regions. Some of the physical phenomena demonstrates that the forces of gravity may be overcome. I have promised to write simply and, therefore, it would be amiss of me to become involved in Newton's dynamics, the electrical theory of matter, effects of inertia and speed, etc. Let me emphasise once again that science must take into account the effects of spirit on mind, of mind on etheric wavelengths and of all these on the world of matter. If minds of living people can truly influence the throwing of dice, then great spiritual minds can influence the energies within the infinite galaxies of God's creation. All the players in the orchestra of life must obey the baton wielded by that infinite mind. Today's scientists are at last discovering that, within the space of every atom, there are minute particles or waves that find matter no obstacle. They have not yet concluded that there are energies not even limited by the speed of light. It is within these energies that life force and spirit reside - in parallel universes of increasing vibrations or levels of consciousness. At some time in the future, science will have to extend its horizon to include the existence and influence of these levels of mind and spirit.

Religion, like science, is still in its infancy for, as in the past, it is still responsible for war, aggression, suppression and ignorance. If man is surrounded by a spiritually influenced world, then it is important that he should understand its workings. We find it strange that religion is still sub-divided into groups, each with their own ideas about life, God and eternity. Ever since man gained his individuality, mind has tried to communicate with those he left behind but, because of indoctrination, communication was attributed to God instead of the invisible world. Those who claimed otherwise were tortured, persecuted and burnt at the stake. We see that, even today, people are executed for trying to impose their religious ideas on others and, although a little progress has been made, it is minimal. Even Spiritualism is divided between those who wish to pay greater tribute to one teacher than another. This is because in our world there are levels of mind that still believe Jesus was the true representative of God and, naturally, impinge their thoughts on earthly minds that are willing to listen.

I repeat once more that those great minds who have a greater understanding of God and creation are in levels beyond both your and our reach. Those of us who are privileged to find a sensitive receiver can only share our knowledge and ideas with that sensitive.

Often the mind of the medium adds to our transmission, so that the listener becomes doubtful as to the origin of those thoughts. This has been, and still is, a handicap in the work of mediums. If telepathic communication on earth ever reaches perfection, then communication from our world to yours would be of the same standard. In the past, mankind should have realised that his communicating ancestors were little different after physical death than before. The same still prevails today, for all communication is from one mind to another of a similar level. Those on earth who seek the truth about our world should seek some earthly elevated mind or learn to listen to themselves. And yet - nobody wants to listen. It would seem in our observation that even those who have become aware of a sixth sense want to use it for either material or monetary gain, or to raise their own self-importance. Such people will only attract those in our world who are of similar mind.

Although, as I said, earthly memories are gradually put to one side, it is of course necessary for us to retain sufficient memory to establish our identity. Many, like myself, thought it would be easy to send back some coded message which might prove our continuity but, because of the difficulties mentioned, we found it nearly impossible. Excuse my sense of humour, but as we tried to transmit the thought "Thursday", the sensitive would claim that they had a communicator who was always thirsty and even add that they enjoyed a drink or two! By the time I tried to establish my survival, mediums of the calibre of Mrs. Piper, Mrs. Leonard, Mrs. Willet and others of similar standard had joined us. Now I realise, more than ever, why Myers' personality was never the same when he tried to communicate with me via the mediumship of Mrs Verrall, Mrs. Holland and the above mentioned. Looking back, it is no wonder that there was difficulty in deciphering the seven envelopes, one inside another, that I left. Had I not left clues, and the final musical five-finger exercise message been successfully received, it would still have been suggested that it was done by clear-seeing - clairvoyance. Is, then, the writer of this book myself or does Raymond have access to all my biographies? Has he ever been inclined to write poetry before? Has he indeed ever written a book before? Why now? The truth is that, only now, in his later years, is he a fit person to become aware of external thoughts and, even then, they are sometimes vague or wrongly expressed.

Miracles were performed by great teachers of the past in the hope that those who saw would listen. Very few did. In my time on earth, there were some wonderful sensitives, yet only a few were convinced of their ability to reach our world. Some earthly minds were able to demonstrate that they could move objects; my friends and I witnessed levitation, but intellect suggested it was no proof of survival. I do agree that good materialisation is very indicative of the survival hypothesis, yet so few people have this gift. Those who did have it would sometimes stoop to fraudulent activities when the energy was low. I refer to my experiences with Eusapia Palladino, as well as other physical mediums. Because of the lack of good physical mediums and the fact that some physical phenomena may be due to the mind of the living, it is realised that other phenomena must be shown before anyone will listen - and yet, even when we learn to place our voice directly on magnetic tape before witnesses, others must rely on their testimony.

Just as, in the past, great teachers and mediums have tried to persuade man of the existence of eternity by miracles and communication, so today a teacher in India does similar miracles, healing and teaching. Again, only a few are willing to listen and yet, slowly the world is becoming aware that life is more than playing, working and having tea. People are more willing to tell of their temporary glimpses of our world; by the advances in medical science, more people have these experiences and can relate them without ridicule. Still reflecting on the past, the sittings with some of those wonderful mediums were not always very satisfactory. Sometimes, Mrs. Piper's control Phinuit would appear to be fishing for information from the sitter and often gave incorrect information. It is no wonder that the lesser-developed mediums of today only excel themselves on odd occasions.

From our observance of your present conditions, it seems that technological advances, especially in visual and audio communication, brought with them an even greater material outlook on life. It also helped to rid religions of their superstitious doctrines, leaving the youth of the present looking for a purpose in life. It is our desire to replace materialism by spirituality, to replace the false doctrines of religion by truth. The invisible world, like radio waves, is all around you, but before you can conceive of its reality, it is necessary to raise the mind's vibrations to those that lie beyond etheric wavelengths - "Spirit-hertz".

Those in higher levels than ourselves, foretell of hope towards the end of this century. They suggest that natural phenomena will sweep the earth clean of garbage, leaving those who respect the planet sufficiently to bring into being a truce between science and religion. As these two forces join hands, it will be realised that everything material and physical is just a necessary school to prepare for that which follows - a mind world - a butterfly world in which the beauty, knowledge and opportunities exceed the wildest imaginings of those who, at this moment, are shackled by the chains of earthly flesh. In the past, man's mind was dominated by religion, politics, tyrants and fear. The mind of man today is not much different. The increase of materialism seems to have increased the mental burden of many who feel they cannot afford to die. Commercialism has become a disease that has crept into the world of mediumship and even the act of dying. The media of wireless, television and newspapers has decided that mankind's interest lies in the more material and sensuous aspects of life. Much of the blame for the actions of modern youth lies with the media, as well as backward religion and corrupt politicians. The only remedy is for people to become more aware of the invisible world, in which exist great minds waiting for man to open his etheric ears to the guidance given, free of charge.

At the moment, the majority of people seem to behave like sheep following political and religious shepherds who, in truth, have only their own welfare in mind. All religions must learn to appreciate the scientific approach to the origin of the earth, life and spirit. Science, in the same way, must learn that there are energies and forces that do not obey the laws within physical science. We as a group implore those who read this book to open their eyes to the design and purpose of earth, birth, life and death; to listen also to the higher thoughts that enter their minds. Not everything can be explained in terms of sub-atomic particles, for there are vibrations of mind that do not even need particles. The higher vibrations of the invisible world use infinite frequencies of a substance that could only be termed "God's essence".

I would like to conclude this chapter by explaining that, having no earthly body, we have no need of earthly food unless our mind demands the etheric counterpart. The same must be said about sexual activities and other pleasures of a physical nature. Only as we progress do we realise that earthly food is replaced by food for the mind and spirit; knowledge and wisdom give a far greater satisfaction than venison. Our thirst is not for wine, women and song, but for the emotional stimulation given by artists, musicians, dance, ballet, opera and other forms of art in which colour, etheric vibrations and spiritual love contribute far more than they ever did in earthly life.

149

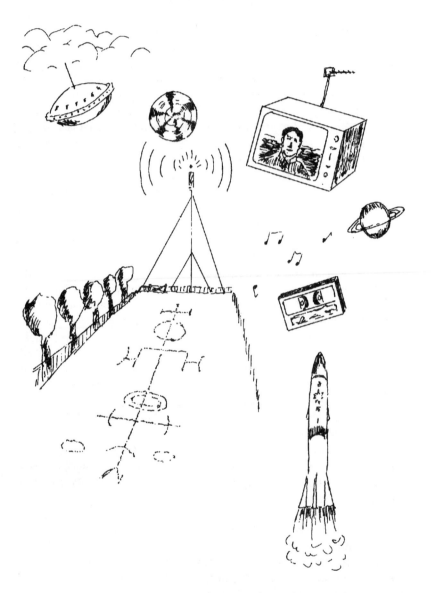

A New Era

Chapter 17

NEW ERA

There is no doubt that, in general, mankind is still steeped in both materialism and superstition - and yet, young people are beginning to put superstition to one side. They are even realising that materialism does not give them the joy, comfort and satisfaction that they seek. The introduction of computer science has brought about another Copernican revolution, facilitating space travel and easier communication, both visual and audible. Travelling from one part of the planet to another is now commonplace, giving a greater realisation that earth is truly but a speck of dust in creation. New phenomena suggest that intelligence is not limited to earth nor even to other planetary surfaces, but pervades and dominates space. Religion still tries to have mankind believe in a personified being, whilst science covers its eyes to anything that is outside the range of physical senses. Many still feel that life must be associated with matter, but include intelligence in their definition of life.

It is true that life needs the complex substance called protoplasm, just as the computer needs its binary system of microchips, but the time approaches when both science and religion combine forces. In this new era will come an acceptance that, just as the computer must be programmed, life needs the guiding principle of intelligence - the higher forms of life needing greater intelligence. It will be known that mind and intelligence do not have to be associated with matter. In fact, in this new age will come a sense of wonder as to how mind and intelligence ever managed to incorporate itself with matter. I know now that this achievement has been the exception rather than the rule, for mind, intelligence and spirit are more at home in inter-planetary cosmic regions than being confined to associating with matter. It would seem appropriate here to quote a poem written, this time, not by my son Raymond, but by one of his brothers:

O body which art free and kind
Be a clean house to hold my mind.
And mind make fair thy rounded bowl
A clean cup to receive my soul.
O soul be still, reflect the far
Clear image of the evening star.

Already in this new age there is the rebirth of physical phenomena although, as my friend Richet would say - no physical phenomena will ever be as convincing as the evidence given by George Pelham. And yet - in order to pull mankind out of the materialistic mud, it will be necessary first of all to present that which appeals to his physical observation. Physical phenomena will therefore be presented by our world, but this time in the light of modern technological advancements. Not only will materialisation take place, but interference with magnetic tapes, television, computers and other electromagnetic machines. There will be such an increase in modern phenomena, that scientists will at last realise that energy exists outside that which is termed matter, to the extent that the higher forms of energy may be termed intelligence. Once this is accepted, there will be less need for physical phenomena. Telepathy will come out of obscurity into reality. Perhaps, then, I will be able to transmit thoughts for another book entitled "For Those Who Are Listening - Hear This".

Humanity is about to move from infancy into youth. It seems to have caught a glimpse of the light at the end of a tunnel. For many, the light is dazzling, so they turn away their eyes, and yet there are some who at least yearn for an understanding of from whence cometh that light. As I have already stated, the time has come for the earth to be swept clean of the garbage within both science and religion, leaving behind those who are capable of leading their companions towards that light. The scientists who probe into those infinite sub-atomic particles will realise that they belong to the same club as the religious leaders who are willing to put superstitions to one side. At the moment, many parents may despair at bringing children into a greedy, selfish and aggressive world. I assure them that, if they encourage their sons and daughters to look beyond the five physical senses, their children will be like caterpillars that have learnt to fly, catching a glimpse of the butterfly world.

I feel now that the reader will profit more if we move on to deal with some more of the enquiries that are transmitted from the mind of this medium between two worlds - the visible and the invisible. Remember that every chapter written relies on the transposition of our thoughts into words. It also relies on our ability to understand those thoughts that he transmits to us. None of us are perfect. We pray that readers have sufficient patience to forgive both his and our imperfections.

Chapter 18

CONCLUSION AND ANSWERS

Before commencing this chapter, it is important once again to stress the fact that communication by telepathic means is limited. From our world to yours requires a medium here and a medium incarnate whose mind, etheric and physical brain all transmit on the same frequency. The programme of any of your computers must be designed to suit the machine through which it gives information. Try to find another living person with whom you may telepathically communicate. We have a similar difficulty. Often in dreams of a more lucid nature, you communicate without the use of voice, gestures or whatever. When the physical body is discarded, telepathic communication becomes more natural, just as it does in dream state. Although we have an etheric body which in a way duplicates the physical, we do not need to use our vocal chords to speak.

We do not need our etheric lungs to breathe, not our etheric heart to beat. In fact, as explained in a previous chapter, we eventually discard even the etheric as we progress into higher levels of mind, yet still communicate with one another, and all in that same level. A torchlight illuminates only a small surface but the sun sheds its light on that hemisphere facing it. I understand that, today, you use light instead of electricity as a means of communication, providing you have some means of interpreting those pulses of light. Magnetic and electric waves pass unimpeded through certain materials, yet find others an obstruction. The grosser particles of an atom find matter an obstruction, yet the finer particles pass easily through it. I use these examples in the hope that you may understand that, in our world, similar conditions prevail. Those in finer or higher levels of mind may easily penetrate the lower, but those in more gross or lower levels find higher levels a natural barrier. Those in the same level of consciousness are on slightly different frequencies, just as in radio waves there are many frequencies on the same wave band. That is why in all levels we work with others whose mental wavelength is only insignificantly different from our own.

In the preceding sentences, I have tried to illustrate the answer to your question "Why is good communication so rare and difficult?" Your mother, father and friends find it very hard to find someone in their level who is on a very close mental frequency to some person in our living world. Occasionally, they find some medium who responds to transmissions of a reasonably close frequency, but not close enough to give truly coherent identity, information and thus definite proof of their continued existence.

Your mind seems to be acknowledging the fact that, in preceding chapters, many of your questions have been answered, yet doubt still manifests in your mental aura. This is your driving force and will be with you until your work is finished. Remember, many make that inevitable journey to our world, yet are not aware of their arrival. They, too, do not want to listen and yet, in truth, they have died. Not only are their etheric ears deaf, but many, because of doubt, do not even see spirit friends who await them. Their mental state is a barrier to the spiritual transmissions of those friends. Search for evidence with open eyes, open ears and, above all, an open mind.

I do realise that, if and when these chapters are published, many will question as to why this channel has been used for reception of our thoughts. If any readers care to do a little research, they will find that we all wished, in earthly life, to establish a differentiation between the physical brain and the mind. Our interests and hobbies were very similar to those of this medium, making him a suitable receptor for our thoughts. "Birds of a feather" - in fact many feathers. Apart from the main interest, an understanding of the mind, it was a common desire of all in our group to prove "life after death". As for earthly common interests, we all had similar pursuits - sport, astronomy and music, combined with a desire to understand all basic principles in science. I have already commented on coincidence and, therefore, ask you to consider whether the fact that this medium has visited Heidelberg, Alassio, Llangollen, Melbourne and many other places that I visited when living, is more than coincidence. His education was similar to mine in the fact that we both had to work hard in order to make progress. He married a lady called Mary - so did I. His main earthly interest is electricity - so was mine. The list of "coincidences" is so long that even the sceptic may accept influences of an external source. One of my sons we named "Raymond". Raymond Lodge and Raymond Smith have names very similar in numerological aspects.

All these factors and many more contribute towards making him a good receiver for our transmissions of thought. Oh, I forgot to mention that he made radios at the age of eleven and used to string up home-made telephones from tree to tree in the woods. Today he is a licensed radio amateur. I suppose that, when I transmitted those first radio waves, I too was a radio amateur, only unlicensed!

In writing these chapters, the group and I have tried not to mention many facts that have been written in other books or biographies. We have endeavoured to explain conditions that prevail in our world of the mind - that world which is a stepping stone to the world of the spirit. There are many things I wrote in my autobiography that I am sure I have forgotten by now, yet realise it is necessary to be able to give enough information to prove my identity. Communication from our world to yours is often as difficult as it is for you to impress the mind of your pet dog, peacock, duck or canary. Franz had a pet canary that used to fly out of its cage onto his shoulder and head. When he died (1815), his friend the canary could not be persuaded even to leave its cage and died not long after Franz came home. This was a case where a human friend was there to meet a non-human friend. The canary stayed as a canary in our world until that time came when both realised that the mind of that canary needed to progress by returning to that level to which it belonged. One could therefore say that death occurs in our levels also, but does not involve physical matter. In the same way, friends in our level of mind make sufficient progress to move onwards to a higher level. We, too, have to say farewell to many whom we love dearly, but with the knowledge that they still survive in a different world. We pray that, in all the preceding chapters, you may have received sufficient understanding of our mind worlds to know that your loved ones now dwell in what is, to most on earth, an invisible world.

In this concluding chapter, we would like to thank all those who have helped our friend Raymond to raise his sensitivity so that he may serve as one of those who have the gift of knowledge and wisdom. Our thanks include all those whom he has met in his life, for from every individual we all learn something. Special thanks go to those who have been patient enough to listen to the initial utterances in early stages. His present wife, June (with the same number of letters as Mary), has become one of our family, since we talk to her daily and, like a group of spiritual vampires, feed on her energy.

Initially, we told this medium that we would write 423 pages and he naturally thought that it would be a long book. It is our intention to write a total of 423 pages, but not all in one book. A praiseworthy medium, not unlike Mrs. Piper, has only recently told our friend that there will be three books. That is our intention, but first it would be wise to see whether anybody wants to listen - and then.

Although through history many thoughts have been added to today's bible through ecclesiastics of old, there are some true philosophies within that book. Those philosophies are common to all the great masters and teachers of both past and present. That great light to whom we are privileged to listen would have me remind you of some of those common truths. "Judge not"; but rather by observing the lack of qualities in others, become more aware of your own shortcomings;. "Do unto others as you would have them do unto you"; if you wish to receive love and understanding then give that love, understanding, sympathy and empathy to everyone that you meet. "Lay up for yourselves treasures of the Spirit rather than treasures on earth"; by accumulating knowledge and wisdom, you gain the power of mind to create that which your mind deserves. We do not need to bring earthly musical instruments, art treasures, silver or gold to invisible dimensions. They are already here waiting for us - here by the creative minds of those in the same level as we find ourselves. The silver and gold are not monetary, but simply colours in greater profusion than ever seen in earthly life. "Love thy neighbour as thyself"; earth is a nursery school where, in its infancy, love is of a physical nature. We love our family, wives or husbands but, in my level I can truly say that the love I have for those in this group is a more refined love than that which I ever knew when in your world. We are in the primary school but have no conception of the love that abounds in God's university.

I now live in the etheric world. The body I now use is composed of etheric substance, but as for understanding that substance, I must confess that I know as much about it as earthly doctors know about life. Just as your medical doctors remedy physical problems of the body, so we here have learnt to control or remedy the etheric by using our minds. Doctors may operate on your earthly bodies, but do not really understand the laws of healing. In similar fashion, we have not learnt all the laws of the mind. By the time we achieve this, I am told that we will not be able to share this knowledge with you.

Once again, we thank you for your patience, asking you to share with all you meet, the fact that you and those here are all on an eternal journey. Some of us are just around the corner, out of sight. The ship that sails out of view is still the same ship which your friends boarded when you said "goodbye". Until we have the pleasure of sharing your company in voice, in song, in words and in love, we here wish you all "good health and happiness".

Goodbye.

O. L. and friends.

POSTSCRIPT

BY JUNE SMITH

Even as a young girl, I used to hear someone call my name - "June, June". It was so real that I would look round to see who was calling and, as a result, often bumped into a lamp post or some person. Unlike my present husband Ray, I somehow always knew inside me that there was another world - a heaven. As a girl, I sang in the church choir and later become a Sunday School teacher. I suppose my early life was similar to Ray's for, in the preface, he mentioned the fact that he also sang in the choir, then became a server. Although very young and inexperienced, I always felt that God was more than just a person; he had to be something much better than just a man. My mother told me the story of how, when she was a little girl in bed with her sisters, she saw a very beautiful lady. Because she was afraid, she hid under the bedclothes but, on peeping out, found the lady had disappeared. It wasn't church or my parents that gave me the assurance of an afterlife. I cannot explain the feeling that I have inside me, I just know there is something else besides my physical life.

On the other hand, Raymond is still searching for that ultimate proof of life after death. Even though he now enters this strange unconscious trance state and listens to the recordings made, he is still not completely convinced of survival. My daughter Annette often sees spirit friends as does her daughter Mia. My son Phillip is a physical medium and, in his presence, tables, trumpets and sandals (all covered with luminous paint) rise in the air. My husband loves to witness this phenomenon but his scientific mind always looks for alternative explanations, even though Phillip and his chair also had luminous strips on them so that we could know exactly where he was in the room.

On one or two occasions when we were sitting with friends, Oliver Lodge told me to place a new audio cassette in Raymond's hands. My husband's face grew red, then purple, and when I was told to play the cassette, Oliver's voice was on it. This sounds unbelievable, but I have living friends who were there when this happened. Raymond's comment was "If Ted Serios could put pictures on a photographic film then maybe I unconsciously put the voice on the cassette." His invisible friends tell me that his doubt is his driving force.

The preface has described how both his hypnosis and trance

state started, so this does not need repeating. Whilst on holiday together in Madeira, Ray went into trance and Frederick (Franz) told me that, if I would lie on the bed and relax, he would try an experiment with me. That was the first time I had ever been hypnotised. During that experience, I had vivid recall of a previous life as a red Indian squaw. I could see the tepees and the elders, particularly my grandmother and, during that lifetime, I used to communicate with my ancestors. When Ray was once conducting a mass hypnosis, I uncovered another life, in which my husband and I bred horses for the purpose of pulling chariots. We were rich and had good business sense. It seems that, in the life I now lead, I have brought with me the experiences I gained in both those lives, for it is always I who buys and sells businesses in this life while Ray uses his knowledge and skills in both maintaining and running them. Apart from my own experiences, I talk to many who have been similarly regressed. I have no doubt whatsoever that reincarnation is a fact.

Ray and I met, not only through the illness of his first wife, but mainly because of our common interest in music - particularly in playing the organ. Ray moved from trumpet to organ after an accident on a motor cycle. I gained my cap and gown certificate on the piano when I was sixteen years old, but later wanted to play the electronic organ. Because of this, we have always used music when sitting in circles. Now, I only have to play a certain cassette and Ray falls into an unconscious state of trance within two or three minutes. This is most useful when he is asked to sit for groups of people, because he is able to link up with his invisible friends in a very short time. Every morning, Ray brings tea to the bedroom. He always drinks his very quickly, then lies down whilst I drink mine slowly. This is the time when no music is necessary. I talk with Oliver, Franz, Phillippe, Ray's dad and even others in the group. They say that his state of trance needs constant use so that it may maintain a high standard. I suppose it is rather like playing the organ - if you don't play constantly, you get out of practice.

Now I feel that Franz, Oliver, Phillippe and Mentor are closer friends of mine than any earthly friends. Oliver is like a father to me, Phillippe a brother, Franz a doctor and Mentor a wise angel. They are all truly wonderful friends. Ray's dad seems only to appear when someone present is contemplating or has contemplated suicide. He explains to them that you cannot run away from responsibilities or challenges in life. Those who do find just as many problems in the invisible world, only of a different nature.

Whenever we are privileged to have a communication from Ray's first wife, it is always me that she talks to. This has shown me, and others, that in her level of mind there is no jealousy, in fact, quite the opposite. It seems that she had to return home so that we could join forces in trying to be of service to others. There seems to be a greater understanding of relationships in the spirit world than there is in physical life. I feel sorry that Ray is so often unconscious and not able to enjoy the communication that I and many friends have with the invisible world - as Oliver describes it. Maybe, sometime in the future, he will be able to witness some phenomenon that will give as much pleasure to him as his trance gives to others.

I cannot write as well as Oliver Lodge or my husband, but swear that all that has been written in the chapters of this book has been received by Ray - from whom? For myself, I know that the personalities who use Ray are real. You must draw your own conclusions. My husband and I have now been together for thirty years. Franz tells me that, all that time, they have been developing him, but I have only been able to speak to his spirit friends during the last ten years. In those ten years, I have made recordings of approximately four hundred hours of trance talks, but there must be at least another four hundred hours that I did not record. When we first met, Ray was a college lecturer - intelligent, good-looking, a music lover and, of course, interested in the psychic world. There were enough common interests and physical attraction to bring us together like two magnets, but he was in those days a little bad-tempered and big-headed. I felt quite sure that, with time, these negative parts of his personality would subside and, if not, maybe I could tame this Leo husband of mine. I did succeed, but not to bear comparison with the effect that the trance state has had on him.

From the moment this phenomena started, I have witnessed a changed person. He is calm and peaceful twenty-four hours a day. No longer does he have a temper, for it seems to me that his mind retains a little of all the personalities who manifest through him, so that I now have a better husband than the one I married. For this I must thank his spirit friends for their influence upon him. For me now it is rather like having one physical husband together with several spirit companions. I pray that they stay with us both until that day comes when our work is done. We can then return to the real world in which they live. In our intimate conversations, Oliver and Phillippe have promised, jokingly, to have the kettle boiling for me! They know how I enjoy a good cup of tea.

To all other ladies who read these words, I would recommend that they persuade their husbands that there is more to life than just the physical pleasures of wine, women and song. The joy and comfort that come from my husband's spirit companions is equal to any pleasure of physical life. I hope and pray that all who read this book may have a glimpse of the knowledge, truth and wisdom that I have gained by listening to them.

Nobody wants to listen - and yet - I do.

Pat Stainsby
14 Strawgate Grove,
Stapleton.
DL2 2RR
JUNE 1996